CORNER OFFICE RULES

THE 10 REALITIES OF EXECUTIVE LIFE

by Keith R. Wyche and
Renee B. Booth Ph.D.

Endorsements

Advance Praise for *Corner Office Rules*

*K*eith Wyche is a proven "Leader of Leaders." The invaluable wisdom he shares in his new book, Corner Office Rules: The Ten Realities of Executive Life, *comes at a time when reaching and staying at the executive level has become more challenging than in any previous time in history. Keith's book provides a clear pathway to meet these new challenges long before they undermine your career aspirations.* —**David Richardson, founder, executive director, National Sales Network**

Corner Office Rules *is for anyone wanting to advance to the C suite. It provides an advance look at the realities they will face and prepares them for success.* —**Mel Parker, president, North America, Brink's, Incorporated**

Keith Wyche's first book, Good Is Not Enough, *helps aspiring executives achieve C-Suite status. His follow-up,* Corner Office Rules, *provides them with the ten key guiding principles necessary to sustain that*

grounded is my inner circle: Curtiss Jacobs; Jon Love; Ron Broadnax; and my executive coach, Kale Evans.

I very much want to acknowledge the special women in my life who have molded me and helped me to grow as a person: my mother, Velvet Wyche; my grandmother, Estella Davis; and my aunts Lois Neyland, Minnie Davis, and Lillian Jones. Last but not least, Denise Wyche-Wells (thanks for getting me through college!), and my "guardian angel," Carla S. Wyche (thanks for getting me through life!).

Renee Bellamy Booth, Ph.D.

I would like to express my deepest thanks and gratitude to my staff and partners at Leadership Solutions, Inc. for their assistance in making this book a reality. They have been steadfast and unwavering in their support of me and their belief in this book and the impact it will have on its readers.

I would also like to thank my coauthor, Keith Wyche, for partnering with me on what has been a great journey as we worked together on this book. Our goal was to share our experiences and ultimately help new leaders navigate executive life in a way that will enhance their leadership experiences. Together, we have achieved this goal.

Finally, I am deeply appreciative of my family for their continued love and support.

Dedications

Keith R. Wyche

This book is dedicated to my children: Alana, Kyle, Kevin, and Angela. Being your father is my highest honor. May you continue to develop the leader within!

Renee Bellamy Booth, Ph.D.

I dedicate this book to my son, Adam who is a reminder to me every day of what is really important in life.

CONTENTS

How This Book Is Structured

Given the pressures of the economy, stakeholder interests, and increased transparency in companies, those selected for top leadership jobs are asked to hit the ground running. In our experience, the skills and characteristics that are critical to being a successful executive are new, challenging, and often counterintuitive. For that reason, coauthor Keith Wyche, who, in his role as the president of ACME Markets (a division of Supervalu), was responsible for the operations of a 113-store, full-service retail and pharmacy chain based in the Philadelphia area with over $2 billion in sales, will share some of the essential truths about the executive experience that are seldom discussed but have the potential to make or break success. His insights are covered in **Part I: Critical Leadership Skills You Must Master (from a Leader's Perspective).**

However, this book is not only about *recognizing* the realities of the executive experience (although anticipation is half the battle). It's about developing strategies to make sure that you are prepared to do the work required of executives—and to thrive while doing so. Renee

Bellamy Booth, PhD, of Leadership Solutions, Inc., a leadership development consulting firm based in Philadelphia, Pennsylvania, is an industrial organizational psychologist specializing in leadership assessment and executive coaching. She shares advice based on her twenty years of coaching C-level executives on managing leadership roles effectively using practical and tested strategies, so that you can *be* the executive you dreamed of becoming. Her insights are covered in **Part II: Managing the Personal Challenges that Come with Leadership (from a Coach's Perspective).**

Introduction: These Rules Will Make You a Better Leader

Contrary to popular opinion, being an executive is not as glamorous as it may seem. Even highly successful leaders are regularly confronted by conflict, criticism, isolation, and self-doubt. The realities of executive life can be sobering for those who are not well prepared for it. But don't be discouraged. We believe that embracing *reality* is essential to achieving personal fulfillment and avoiding disillusionment. We don't need to argue that becoming an executive is an amazing opportunity; you already know it is. What we cover in this book is the importance of managing the distractions that can interfere with your ability to maximize the experience.

Drawing on our more than fifty years of combined experience in senior leadership roles and as coaches to leaders, this book illustrates the ten most profound realities of executive life. These realities are often unspoken or misunderstood, and if they're ignored, they have the potential to bring major consequences. Understanding them will prepare new executives—or anyone functioning in a senior leadership capacity—to put things in perspective, feel more satisfied, and make a lasting impact on an organization while avoiding common pitfalls.

From mentorship to corporate management training to MBA programs, there is no shortage of access to preparation for those entering first-line manager jobs. It is widely recognized that being a successful manager requires a skill set that is separate from that needed to be an individual contributor. Following this logic, we expect to find developmental resources for aspiring executives as well. After all, leading at the executive level is clearly full of unique demands, surprises, and traps. Yet, it turns out that there is very little guidance available to new executives about the practical realities of what being an executive is really like.

Asking a seasoned professional to sink or swim at the most visible and competitive level of the organization hardly seems fair or practical. Certainly, business journals offer numerous articles explaining how to effectively execute the job—how to motivate, innovate, network, and so on—but none of this material accurately portrays the *experience* of being an executive.

There are a few reasons why there aren't more honest accounts detailing what it's like to be an executive. For starters, no one wants to be perceived as a cynic or a "dream killer." Furthermore, it's easier to talk about skills and attributes that should exist in a perfect world. Describing reality requires incredible insights, hands-on experience, and keen observation of the subtle details that differentiate success and failure. These kinds of observations can only be made in the executive suite and do not typically emerge in traditional training environments.

In the absence of honest descriptions about the realities of executive life, aspiring leaders are left to adopt an outsider's view of the executive suite. The life-changing benefits of becoming an executive are well documented. Executives enjoy numerous business and personal incentives that our society celebrates. While power, wealth, and influence are products of becoming an executive, none of these material outcomes describe what the experience *feels* like.

Without proper preparation and conditioning, new executives are inevitably shocked to discover that the actual challenges are a far cry from what they had imagined. Consider the following example:

New Executive Discovers Unforeseen Challenges

Six months ago, Don was named chief financial officer (CFO) of Biomedix, a pharmaceutical company. Prior to joining the management team, Don had successfully climbed the ranks in various finance-related roles, including business planning and portfolio management. Just before joining Biomedix, Don had spent thirteen years in finance functions for a major beverage company. His leadership responsibilities so far had mostly entailed managing compact teams of highly skilled specialists.

For Don, the promotion to CFO was a dream come true. Immediately, he thought of how his life would change for the better. Having been raised with modest means, this opportunity marked a significant landmark for his entire family. Don felt that, finally, his years of hard work and dedication had been recognized. Being familiar with the functional parameters of the CFO role, Don was confident in his ability to master the position just as he had mastered other jobs in the past—with an open mind, a collaborative spirit, and the drive to achieve results.

Don's first few months as an executive were a challenge, to be sure. He fully expected to encounter increased pressure, delicate politics, and a sharp learning curve. But Don's concerns were more nuanced than that. Immediately, some of his former peers started treating Don differently, as if he had suddenly acquired superpowers. But as a newcomer, Don felt less *powerful than before. And to his dismay, Don started hearing whispers that he had undermined another colleague to win the job.*

To make matters worse, the executive team meetings were often confrontational, and he felt awkward engaging in conflict with his former bosses, now turned peers. In Don's highly analytical area of expertise, the best solution regularly emerged organically, and his direct reports rarely argued or bullied each other. He expected the executive team to be just that: a team*—of collaborative, open-minded, and inclusive professionals. And the back-channel conversations surrounding meetings were another matter altogether. It was as if the private conversations* *preceding and following meetings were more decisive than the formal meetings themselves.*

After three months on the job, Don figured that the learning curve would flatten and things would get easier. Instead, he found himself faced with another set of unexpected challenges. For instance, Don was used to taking his privacy and anonymity for granted. Before, no one had ever cared enough to notice that he was a gun enthusiast who enjoyed going to a firing range after work. But now, he was beginning to feel as if every aspect of his life was subject to scrutiny, especially with the rise of the Internet. Photographs of his house could be found on Trulia and of his family on Facebook, and even a fifty-dollar political contribution he had made ten years ago could be revealed in a Google search.

The work was getting harder, too. In the past, Don would respond to pressure by hunkering down and focusing on results. However, his fellow executives appeared more readily influenced by relationships than by sheer metrics. Don lacked experience with this kind of persuasion since he had always preferred to let his numbers do the talking. To compound his struggles, Don found that he had no one to confide in. His work had become too sensitive to share with his direct reports, and most of his new peers didn't understand the specifics of his function since it fell beyond the scope of pharmaceutical products, per se. Six months into his dream job, Don felt disillusioned. He wondered how this golden opportunity had started to slip from his grasp so quickly.

Because the roles of senior management are relatively elusive, it's no surprise that professionals are more focused on achieving the position rather than actually understanding what the job entails. Most aspiring leaders actively plan and strategize how to become an executive as if it were an end result, like reaching a mountaintop. Successfully getting to the top requires a blend of talents and conditions, including tenacity, capability, patience, agility, and luck. While the topic of advancement has mass appeal for those seeking the proverbial "roadmap for success," learning the steps to get there does little to illuminate the realities of the executive experience. In the following chapters, we encourage professionals to spend as much effort preparing to succeed as an executive as they do trying to secure the opportunity.

PART I

CRITICAL LEADERSHIP SKILLS YOU MUST MASTER (FROM A LEADER'S PERSPECTIVE)

BY KEITH R. WYCHE

REALITY 1

WHAT MADE YOU SUCCESSFUL *THEN,* WON'T *NOW*
It's a Different Ball Game at the Top!

Several years ago, I had the great privilege of being named senior vice president (SVP) of a Fortune 500 organization. I had worked my way up the ladder. Beginning as an entry-level sales executive, I had earned promotions to positions of increased responsibility, from sales representative to sales manager to sales director. Along the way, I had great mentors who encouraged me to grow as a professional by expanding my skill set. This led to me taking strategic lateral positions to gain operational experience and profit-and-loss (P&L) responsibility. With these new experiences, I moved into general manager roles and later into vice president (VP) positions. After roughly twenty years of working in key roles for major organizations, delivering great results at every level, I was poised and ready to become a senior leader...or so I thought!

For the first half of my career, my success was driven primarily by performance, hard work, a focus on details, and delivery of results. To enhance my effectiveness, I worked hard at being a "likeable" leader whose elevator speech was: "I am a professional. I have no problems; I create no problems. I only *solve* problems." As I began to manage teams, I was able to motivate them to meet and exceed the expectations of the organization. If by chance a team struggled, I had no problem micromanaging or even taking over the tasks assigned to direct reports to get the job done. In essence, my formula for success was, "Deliver results (even if you have to do it yourself). Be well liked by your bosses, and effectively manage those under you to get the job done." Stepping into the SVP role, I was confident that this playbook, which had served me so well to this point, would lead me to even greater success. What I quickly learned was that the focus on execution and results that had made me successful early on often got in the way of the nuanced behaviors that are required to lead at the executive level. This concept may sound counterintuitive; we are essentially saying that what got you to the executive floor won't be enough to keep you there.

WHAT IS DIFFERENT FOR AN EXECUTIVE LEADER?

As an executive, you spend more time listening and less time talking. Instead of solving problems yourself, you must learn to ask the right questions that lead others to solve them. Rather than just manage down within your organization to deliver results, you need to manage across and manage up to accomplish your goals. Last, instead of likability, your credibility and integrity are the calling cards required to drive the influence and collaboration you need to get results.

At this point you may be saying, "It sounds like I'll spend a lot of time and energy in conversation," and you would be correct. As a senior leader, you'll spend significantly more time in meetings, on conference calls, and getting employee and customer feedback than ever before. Some days, you will wonder if you did any measurable work at all! But the work of an executive is to ensure that the organization remains engaged, motivated, committed, and focused on achieving its goal. This is not to imply that hard work and delivering results are no longer essential to success. You just need to recognize that *how* you work will be different, and results will be the by-product of your effectiveness at executive tasks. The complex challenge of executive leadership does not allow you to simply rely on your fallback skills. Instead, you must develop and leverage new skills that may fall outside your sweet spot.

We have found that many new executives are surprised to learn that the following skills, while important, are in *less* demand within the executive suite:

- **Likability:** As we've said, being well liked may translate into success at lower levels of the organization, but sheer popularity is not enough to persuade and impact other executives. Credibility and indirect influence are more likely to get results at the top.

- **Doing it all yourself:** As an individual contributor or producing manager, to get results, you may find it necessary to micromanage at times or even to take over the tasks of direct reports. However, an executive no longer has the flexibility or the personal power to take on the work of others. Instead, an executive is expected to get work done through others by providing a clear vision, motivating staff, and selecting the right people to execute on his or her behalf.

- **Managing down:** While a manager is expected to maintain close, familiar relationships with direct reports, an executive may not have access or time to connect with what is often a large staff. It is critical that you learn how to *manage up and across* to forge new relationships with your peers, your bosses' peers, your external counterparts (i.e., vendors, suppliers, customers), and in some cases, the media, board members, and government officials.

Conversely, we have found that many new executives are surprised to learn that the following skills are in *more* demand within the executive suite:

- **Listening**
- **Questioning**
- **Empowering**

- **Partnering**
- **Recognizing and Rewarding**

Later in this chapter, we discuss the importance of honing and developing these new keys to success as a senior leader.

WHY IS IT DIFFERENT FOR AN EXECUTIVE LEADER?

Earlier in your career, the focus was most likely on achieving results on an individual or department level. Most of the resources you needed were at your disposal, you controlled much of the decision making, and external factors were considered out of your control. However, as an executive leader, you face new realities:

Your focus is on the success of the organization: As a senior-level executive, your efforts will no longer focus solely on the results of your team, department, or division. Your focus will be on how the success of your team, department, or division can contribute to the overall success of the organization. In fact, at this level, a portion of your compensation is typically tied to the success of the organization. You will need to think "organization first" rather than what's best for you and your team. For some, this can be a difficult transition to make. If an executive leader struggles or refuses to make it, it can severely hinder his or her effectiveness and diminish the results of the overall operation.

I witnessed firsthand how such a mindset can drive an organization's overall performance. I once served as one of several division presidents in a Fortune 50 organization. The board of directors realized that to be more competitive, it was essential that it make strategic price investments in our product offerings. This suggestion was challenging, because funds were limited. We could either allocate the price investment funds equally among all the divisions, or we could choose to invest in the division(s) that would yield the greatest return on investment (ROI). If the vote was to allocate the funds based on ROI, many divisions would not receive any price investment. However, by dividing the funds equally, no one division would receive enough investment to make a meaningful impact. Correctly, the presidents decided to allocate every dollar to the division that would yield the greatest return. While this was a difficult decision, the reality is that it meaningfully improved the performance of the organization as a whole.

You need to be more strategic than tactical: As a mid-level executive, most of your energy and effort was directed toward the accomplishment of quarterly or yearly goals. Due to the dynamic nature of doing business in the twenty-first century, the rate of change forces you to stay nimble as you react to shifts in the economy, industry, and other unpredictable factors. The challenge of operating in this manner as a senior leader is that you "can't see the forest for the trees." In other words, you are playing checkers when you need to be playing chess. In addition to focusing on your next move, your next product, or your next quarter's results, you need to consider several moves ahead:

- Where is the industry moving?
- How are consumer habits changing?
- How can we leverage technology?
- Who are our new competitors, and how do we combat them?

Failure to look at the bigger picture strategically has negatively impacted many companies and even industries:

- *Video rental stores:* Were technology advancements that helped create video streaming, Netflix, and Redbox anticipated?
- *Stand-alone bookstores:* With the launch of Amazon.com, e-books, and the Kindle, did these organizations do enough to compete?
- *Grocery retail:* Was enough thought given to the influx of specialty retailers such as Whole Foods, Trader Joe's, or Wegmans? Was there a plan to compete with discount grocers such as ALDI, the dollar stores, and Save-a-Lot?

These are but a few examples that highlight the need for executives to maintain a balance between managing the tactical *and* the strategic.

For new executive leaders, this reality must be embraced sooner rather than later.

You must receive and interpret data from multiple vantage points: To think and act truly strategically, executive leaders need to integrate information from multiple sources. No longer can you limit your data points to a vital few. You will have to gain perspectives from many constituents: customers, vendors, employees, thought leaders, and even competitors. Making decisions in a vacuum or relying only on internal sources of information limits your perspective and may hinder your organization's effectiveness. As an executive leader, you need to draw upon your listening skills and ask the questions that enhance your ability to make sound decisions.

THE IMPORTANCE OF DIVERSE INSIGHTS

In December of 2009, I was named president of Cub Foods, a $3 billion grocery retailer operating in the Twin Cities of Minneapolis and St. Paul. Being brand-new to the grocery business, I met with my new leadership team to understand the key drivers for success. My leadership team was made up of lifelong grocery executives who had started in the industry literally as kids bagging groceries and stacking cans. They were extremely knowledgeable about grocery store operations and took time to teach me *the business. In their opinion, success for Cub would come through great product selection, competitive prices, "hot" ads in the weekly circulars, and massive merchandise displays that shouted "value" to our customers.*

Although I agreed with the success factors my team shared with me, I wanted to hear more; my inquisitive nature led me to seek input from external sources. I set out to listen to and question others regarding how Cub could improve its performance. Here are some key groups I spoke with and the issues I learned about by not limiting my source of information to my internal team:

- **Millennials:** *This group shared with me that since we only adver-tised in newspapers and mailers, we were not likely to reach them; therefore, they were more likely to shop elsewhere. They encour-aged us to create smartphone apps, a Facebook page, and online coupons; they also taught us how to use Twitter to generate sales.*
- **Vendors:** *I was amazed at the amount of analytical information our vendors had about my customers. I learned about the importance of providing gluten-free products, the popularity of Greek yogurt, and the need to provide more organic produce, as a large segment of the population was focused on eating healthier.*
- **Thought Leaders:** *Given that most leaders in the grocery busi-ness are men but 85 percent of grocery shoppers are women, I wanted to hear from someone who could give me a woman's per-spective. I brought in Bridget Brennan, author of the best-selling*

book Why She Buys *as a speaker for my leadership team. In a few hours, Bridget was able to convey to my predominantly male audience how to effectively merchandise and market to our largest customer segment. Her insights helped us create "Project SHE (Simplify Her Experience)." It greatly improved the shopping experience in our stores. One great example of what we learned was that women shoppers gauged the cleanliness of our store by the cleanliness of the ladies' restroom. Additionally, we lowered our shelves to make our products more accessible when we learned that the average woman was five feet, four inches tall. Some of our shelves were over six feet high.*

- **Customers:** *For the same meeting, I invited a panel of current Cub customers to share with my entire organization what they liked and didn't like about Cub. Much of what they shared was positive; however, we learned how we could improve our produce, enhance our customer service, provide more functional shopping carts, and improve the check-out experience.*

By creating a strategy that integrated the knowledge of my team with the insights we gained by listening to our millennials, vendors, thought leaders, and customers, Cub was able to achieve double-digit sales growth in year one! There is no doubt in my mind that such a feat could not have been accomplished without the valuable input from external sources.

YOU MUST RELY ON OTHERS TO SUCCEED

As your responsibilities and span of control increase, you quickly lose the ability to "make" things happen on your own. In today's world of matrix organizations, dotted-line reporting, and decentralized decision making, executives just don't have the bandwidth or the expertise to make such high-stakes, complex decisions alone. You can't know it all, you can't do it all, and you can't manage it all. To succeed, you'll need to rely on peers, subordinates, your leadership team, board members, and others.

As opposed to the skills that made you a success early in your career, you will need to add and develop the following:

- **Listening:** An old proverb says that we were born with one mouth and two ears so that we might listen twice as much as we talk. As an executive leader, it is essential that you develop your listening skills. And never confuse hearing with listening. Many of us hear, but we don't listen. Listening requires focusing on what others are saying, giving them your full attention, and absorbing what is said. Furthermore, you should listen every chance you get. Listen to your peers, listen to your customers and former customers, listen to your associates, and even listen to your critics.

- **Questioning:** Although listening is essential, it is equally important that you develop questioning skills. Very often, when listening to others it's easy to assume you understand what they are saying. We believe it's possible to gain even richer insights by asking the right questions. When in doubt, just ask, "Why?" Such questioning gives the speaker an opportunity to provide the logic and reasoning behind his or her comment or recommendation and helps the leader better synthesize the information.

- **Empowering:** By empowering others, you accomplish several worthwhile tasks:

  o You free up your time, which allows you to address more critical matters.

  o You help others to develop and grow by providing them with opportunities to stretch and grow their skills. You teach them *how* to fish instead of fishing for them.

  o You create a sense of teamwork and accountability by sharing responsibility among team members and by making expectations clear.

  o You cultivate a "can-do" culture where everyone feels valued because everyone contributes.

- **Partnering:** As an executive, you need to partner with peers and others in the organization to get things done. You set the organization on a path for success by creating an atmosphere of collaboration, since you understand that organization success trumps individual success.

- **Recognizing and Rewarding:** Because most executive leaders are focused on driving the organization to meet its goals, many times they fail to recognize and reward those whose efforts make achieving such goals possible. We forget that at the end of the day, we are all people, and people have a need to feel valued and appreciated. In my experience, the acknowledgment of a job well done, whether with a handwritten letter of thanks or even a simple phone call, can make an individual or department perform at even higher levels just because they feel valued. Remember, people don't care how much you know until they know how much you care!

REALITY 2

You Don't Know Everything
Using Your Team to Help You Learn What You Don't Know

_____

$\mathbf{Y}$ou've finally reached the top of the ladder! Your title may be CEO, CFO, president, executive vice president, senior vice president, partner, or some other prestigious corporate title. Perhaps you are a leader in other arenas and carry the title of executive director, principal, pastor, dean, captain, coach, business owner, or chairperson. Your constituents may call you mayor, governor, senator, or even president. Regardless of your title, *you* are the person in charge. The buck stops with you. The failure or success of your business or organization rests on *your* shoulders. Furthermore, everyone (and I do mean *everyone*!) looks to you for direction, leadership, and advice.

The expectations others place on you (not to mention the ones you place on yourself) demand that you notice all the headwinds, craft all the solutions, anticipate all the problems, listen to all the questions, and most of all...provide all the answers. You have an entire grandstand of people focused on *you*: customers, board members, congregants, subordinates, shareholders, constituents, clients, colleagues, students, and sometimes even the media. In most cases, the people in the grandstand offer problems with no solutions, questions with no answers, demands with no alternatives, and arguments with few, if any, facts.

Welcome to the world of senior leadership! You are no longer that middle manager who can hide behind the bosses; you *are* the boss! No longer can you point to "unforeseen factors" as the reason for your inability to achieve your objectives. It's *your* business, your organization, your team, and *your problem*. But if you allow the unrealistic expectations of others (or yourself) to dictate your agenda, you will never please anyone, solve anything, or deliver on any goals. To perform effectively as a senior leader, you must accept the reality that *you'll never have all the answers*.

LOU GERSTNER'S ADVICE

In 1993, I was an associate at IBM during a time of crisis for the company. Our former beloved CEO, John Akers, had retired and was replaced by industry unknown Lou Gerstner. Concerning to most IBMers was the fact that Gerstner did not have a background in computers, software, or anything to do with the fast-paced, research-and-development-intensive world of information technology. Gerstner had recently served as chairman and CEO of RJR Nabisco and previously had spent eleven years at American Express. Hardly the person IBMers expected to lead the company in troubling times! Many wondered if IBM would even survive. But during Gerstner's tenure, not only did the company survive, it thrived.

By the time Gerstner stepped down in 2002, the company had totally reinvented itself. It had gone from being a manufacturer of computer hardware, software, and peripherals to a services provider focused on business consulting. Rather than assuming he had all of the answers, Gerstner relied on the insight and advice of others inside the company. A *Harvard Business Review* article quoted Gerstner: "People at IBM were very smart. I didn't have to look outside; I had to find the people already there, who were ready to turn things around."[1]

ATTRACT, EMPOWER, AND RETAIN THE BEST TALENT

As a leader, once you wrap your head around the idea that you don't have all of the answers, you will quickly come to the realization that you need to find others who can help you arrive at the best answers. Make

---

[1] Lagace, Martha. "Gerstner: Changing Culture at IBM—Lou Gerstner Discusses Changing the Culture at IBM," *Harvard Business Review*, December 9, 2012. http://hbswk.hbs.edu/archive/3209.html.

no mistake about it: the most important asset of any organization is its human capital—its *people*. Show me a high-performing team in any industry or space, and I'll show you a team made up of winners. Neither leaders nor organizations rise above the level of talent on its roster. You may experience momentary glimpses of success and prosperity with a mediocre team, but sustained growth and improvement require the collective input of talented individuals.

Please know that attracting top talent requires more than a big office, a hefty signing bonus, or a lofty title. Talented individuals relish the opportunity to *display* their talent. They do not enjoy working in micromanaged environments; neither do they thrive just implementing someone else's plan. The people who will help you lead the organization want a seat at the table, a voice in the discussion, and the ability to influence the vote. To attract them, you must sell them on your vision and the meaningful roles they can play in accomplishing it. To develop and get the best out of them, you must empower them to make decisions and take risks. And to retain them, you must challenge them with greater opportunities to grow.

PRESIDENT REAGAN DID IT RIGHT!

Our fortieth president, actor-turned-politician Ronald Wilson Reagan, was a master at surrounding himself with the best talents and letting them do what they do best. Beginning with his selection of George Bush as his vice-presidential running mate in 1980, President Reagan recruited a team that would help him restore the nation's self-confidence.

One such team member was Murray Weidenbaum, who served as Reagan's first chairman of the Council of Economic Advisers. In a 2006 Directors & Boards Magazine *article[2], Weidenbaum referred to the president as a "gifted executive" and shared three of the many leadership traits that made Reagan successful:*

1. *Set clear and attainable objectives (even if they seem difficult to achieve)*
2. *Choose subordinates who share your views and outlook*
3. *Give your people lots of leeway and operating authority*

According to Weidenbaum, "those of us who put together the budget cuts had full discretion in assembling an ambitious assortment of spending reductions. Subsequently, President Reagan sat down with us and reviewed each significant budget change before making the final decision. He was anything but a rubber stamp. He did not try to micromanage the decision making within each of our agencies, but he held us accountable for the results. He empowered us to exercise a lot of discretion."[3]

---

[2] Weidenbaum, Murray. "The management style of Ronald Reagan: there is much to learn from this unusually gifted chief executive. Here are my 10 lessons." *Directors & Boards* 31 (2006): Pg. 87.
[3] Ibid.

YOU'VE ACHIEVED SUCCESS, NOT PERFECTION

The fact that you are serving in a leadership capacity speaks volumes about what you've been able to accomplish in your given field. Considering the fact that the higher you climb, the narrower the pyramid, you've excelled above all your challenges, competitors, and colleagues. Along the way, you've honed your leadership skills by successfully managing and leading people and organizations. You've been awarded, recognized, written about, and touted for your achievements. By all accounts, you are the complete leader. However, I must remind you of this very important fact: you've achieved success, not perfection!

As leaders, we too often allow our strengths to become our weaknesses. We know the hard work, blood, sweat, and tears we shed to get to this point in our careers. We've had to solve all sorts of problems, meet extremely tight deadlines, and deliver on results. We know our way works! But if we are honest with ourselves, we've also made our share of mistakes along the way. We've missed deadlines, didn't hit objectives, blown big presentations, made bad hiring decisions…the list goes on. In fact, we've learned more from our failures than our successes. In other words, it is essential that you recognize that not only is your way *not* the only way, but that your way was full of mistakes. And, since *you* learned by making mistakes, you must allow others the same learning opportunity.

AN IVY LEAGUER'S "MY WAY
OR THE HIGHWAY" MISTAKE

It seemed like the perfect match. A highly recruited corporate professional with an Ivy League pedigree was named executive director of a major nonprofit organization. Helen was a unanimous pick by the board of directors. They had been looking for a candidate who could bring the best practices of the Fortune 500 to revitalize their organization and take it to the next level, and all indications were that Helen fit the bill.

As expected, she hit the ground running. By her first presentation to the board, she had identified the organization's key strengths and challenges. Her strengths, weaknesses, opportunities, and threats (SWOT) analysis was thorough and clearly detailed what steps the organization needed to take to realize its mission. However, during the question-and-answer period, a board member challenged her assumptions, and she became extremely defensive. Later, she totally dismissed a suggestion offered by another board member.

After that meeting, the chairman met with Helen to offer some advice: "It's great that you have put so much thought into your plans. But I need you to be open to feedback, ready for pushback, and willing to embrace the ideas of others. We don't expect you to know everything or have all the answers." As a result of that conversation, Helen became a more effective leader who incorporated the ideas of others and worked more collaboratively. More important, she was relieved of the pressure to be the "perfect" leader.

YOU ARE STILL A WORK IN PROGRESS

In his book *On Competition*, Michael E. Porter dedicated an entire chapter to "The Seven Things That Surprise New CEOs." One of his most sobering recognitions was that "most new chief executives are taken aback by the unexpected and unfamiliar new roles, the time and information limitations, and the altered professional relationships they run up against."[4] Porter's co-author Nitin Nohria, the current dean of Harvard Business School who is credited with overhauling the college's competitive MBA program, admits there are challenges that come along with being a CEO. In a 2011 *Fortune Magazine* article entitled, "Harvard Biz School's Extreme Makeover," reporter John Bynre quotes Nohria as saying, "It's not a job that you are ever ready for. Some would say it's ironic that I should be surprised and yet in many ways I had that same surprise."[5]

---

[4] Porter, Michael E. *On Competition*, updated and expanded edition. Boston: Harvard Business School Publishing, 2008. Pg. 523.

[5] Byrne, John. "Harvard Biz School's Extreme Makeover," *Fortune Magazine*, June 30, 2011. http://management.fortune.cnn.com/2011/06/30/harvard-business-school-extreme-makeover/?section=magazines_fortune&utm_source=feedburner&utm_medium=feed&utm_campaign=Feed%3A+rss%2Fmagazines_fortune+%28Fortune+Magazine%29.

The truth of the matter is, most senior leaders are given their new roles because of their accomplishments in lesser roles, not because they have displayed all the skills required to excel in the new job. Said differently, most of us are promoted on potential. We have demonstrated an ability to get results in the past and have convinced the board, executive management, the superintendent, or the voters that we have what it takes to deliver the same level of success in the future in more complex leadership roles. However (assuming that there is no perfect candidate), we all need to realize that every new senior leader has a few blind spots—areas in which he or she is either unskilled or lacks significant expertise to effectively accomplish all expectations of the role. Such blind spots may be due to limited exposure to certain functional areas (e.g., mergers and acquisitions, supply chain, or international business) or due to weakness in the "soft" skills areas of public speaking, interpersonal communication, or general people management. Whatever the shortcoming, it's essential that a leader is self-aware enough to understand where he or she is lacking and is committed to continuous improvement. Many a senior leader has had a career derailed by ignoring or downplaying the need for continuous growth.

COACH BELICHICK'S SHAKY START

Today, if you were asked to name the most successful National Football League coaches of all time, no doubt the name Bill Belichick would be at or near the top of the list. As head coach of the NFL's New England Patriots, he has led his teams to over twenty-three play-off appearances, played in five Super Bowls (winning three), and been named Associated Press Coach of the Year three times. By any measure, Coach Belichick is the example of a successful leader. More of his accomplishments include developing six of his assistant coaches into NFL head coaches, including Romeo Crennel, Eric Mangini, and Nick Saban. Six of his assistant coaches have gone on to become NCAA Division I head coaches. Others credit Coach Belichick as helping them develop into head coach material. Such success might lead one to believe that Belichick has always been a great head coach. However, there are fans in Cleveland who remember a different Bill Belichick.

Belichick came to the Cleveland Browns as head coach in 1991, replacing Bud Carson. As a Bill Parcells protégé, it was expected that he would return the franchise to its glory days. What happened after his arrival was anything but glorious. In his ESPN story entitled "To Understand Belichick, look what he did with Browns," Gene Wojciechowski quoted newspaper reporter Mary Kay Cabot as saying, "There were mistakes he made here on players, personnel, staff, and public relations."[6] He demanded that local hero and Browns quarterback, Bernie Kosar, be released during the middle of the 1993 season.

---

[6] Wojciechowski, Gene. "To Understand Belichick, look what he did with Browns," *ESPN*, January 27, 2008. http://sports.espn.go.com/espn/columns/story?columnist=wojciechowski_gene&id=3217121&sportCat=nfl

His aloof style and reluctance to be interviewed by reporters earned him the name "Dr. Doom." Belichick himself admitted that his time in Cleveland was less than stellar. In his book The GM, *a riveting story chronicling the biggest highs and lows in NFL history, author Tom Callahan recounts Belichick's admission of failure to Browns' general manager Ernie Accorsi, "I really screwed up that thing up in Cleveland, Ernie."[7]*

On Valentine's Day 1996, after five seasons and a 36–44 record, Belichick received a call from team owner Art Modell informing him that his services were no longer needed. Instead of fading into obscurity, Belichick worked to reinvent himself and learn from his lessons in Cleveland. He worked under Parcells again as an assistant head coach with the Patriots, and later with the New York Jets. In fact, he was prepared to succeed Parcells as coach of the Jets, but New England courted him, and Belichick became the Patriots' head coach in 2000. The rest, as they say, is history. Taking the lessons he learned in Cleveland, he was better able to communicate with the media, motivate veteran players (e.g., Corey Dillon and Randy Moss), and connect with the fans. Make no mistake about it—he's still not known as a "people person," but he has become one of the winningest coaches in NFL history.

---

[7] Callahan, Tom. *The GM: A Football Life, a Final Season, and a Last Laugh.* New York: Random House, 2008. Pg. 80.

NEW ROLE, NEW ORGANIZATION = NEW LEARNINGS

You might assume that on some level, once you reach the senior leadership ranks, a leader is a leader is a leader; the skills you've developed are transferable; and that leading one organization is very similar to leading another. A balance sheet is a balance sheet, a P&L is a P&L, and a staff is a staff. Right? There may be subtle differences in the industries in which you've worked, but you've been successful in the past. Furthermore, you were hired to be a "change agent" who could leverage your skills to transform the organization, and as such, your fresh ideas will be received and embraced, your questioning of the culture will be viewed as refreshing, and your new team will be eager to follow your leadership. Right? Well, maybe. But more than likely, you'll discover that joining a new organization, even as a senior leader, brings its own unique challenges and learnings.

For starters, quite often the phrase "we hired you to be a change agent" really means, "we may want you to be a change agent, but we want you to do it *our* way." Organizations, like people, can be extremely averse to change. They have their rituals, their sacred cows, and their golden boys and girls, and you must be aware of them all. In all honesty, they really *do* want change. They realize that what worked in the past is no longer working, yet they may still be reluctant to let go of the past. They know they need to change, yet they just don't know how!

They do acknowledge that your diverse background and experiences are why they hired you, but because you were not "born and raised" in their company or industry, your initial ideas and suggestions tend to get discounted.

GIVE US YOUR EARLY OBSERVATIONS...KINDA SORTA

I had the opportunity to experience this phenomenon firsthand when I joined Pitney Bowes in the fall of 2003 as area vice president of western operations for the Mailing Systems Division. In this role, I was responsible for running half of Pitney's cash cow: its US mailing operations. I had no experience in the mailing industry, but I had a track record of success in running sales, operations, and call centers for companies like IBM, Convergys, and AT&T. I was recruited to help transform the twelve-hundred-strong sales organization into a more "solutions-based" sales organization, as opposed to the "box" selling they had done for years. With literally thousands of customers ranging from the local dentist to Fortune 100 companies, I was tasked with taking cost out of the business while driving return on sales.

After ninety days on the job, I was asked to present to my boss and the chief operations officer (COO) what observations I had thus far. I put together a PowerPoint presentation that challenged our existing "go-to-market" strategy. I suggested that we could be more profitable if we focused our outside sales team on our larger customers and serviced the smaller ones (the bulk of our customers) in a call center environment utilizing inside sales reps. I detailed how we could cut the number of outside sales reps in half, reduce the overall number of VPs and district offices, and drive sales by focusing our best reps on our largest customers, segmented by industry. In my mind, it was a compelling, well-thought-out presentation. However, my COO bristled and stated, "I think we need more feet on the street, not less, if we are going to drive sales." He added, "And I can't imagine selling mailing equipment from a call center. Customers want to see a live person." While I couldn't disagree more, I was astute enough to know not to challenge him on this matter. Instead, I provided examples of how other companies, like Dell and CDW, were successful using my proposed model and asked if I could pilot a small project to prove or disprove my ideas.

To his credit, the COO allowed me to test my theory in the Seattle/Spokane area (albeit reluctantly). Using a small inside sales team, we were able to outsell the large outside sales team ten to one. A few years later, the entire Pitney mailing sales organization was restructured to look very similar to what I had first suggested, and the number of VPs and district offices were cut significantly. A key learning for me was understanding that in a new organization, one may need to pilot one's new ideas to gain support. I also learned that it can be very important to include best practices of successful companies to help build support for an argument.

CULTURE IS KING...NOT YOU!

Every industry has its own culture, and so does every company, even within the same industry. Silicon Valley behaves much differently than Wall Street. Nordstrom executes totally differently from Sears, and nonprofits function at a totally different level from that of their Fortune 1000 counterparts. In my book *Good Is Not Enough*, I spent a great deal of time sharing with readers the importance of understanding the culture of the company they go to work for, ideally *before* they join the organization. The discussion focused on the fact that you are more likely to be successful if you understand the culture and are able to adapt accordingly. The message was targeted to young professionals aspiring to climb the corporate ladder. What I neglected to mention is that even when you have climbed that ladder and are calling the shots, your success in a new role, department, or organization still depends on how well you navigate the culture.

No matter how accomplished you are, you can never underestimate the impact of organizational culture. It can stifle the best of transformations, cripple the best strategic plans, and paralyze the most nimble of organizations. Even though you may be the leader, your lofty title does not exempt you from the need to understand your organization's culture. Is the organization dominated by a particular business unit (e.g., operations versus sales)? Are promotions primarily internal versus outside hires? Are workers empowered to act according to their best judgment, or are they merely robots who only perform what is asked? Does the organization embrace risk taking, or does it just toe the line? Do senior leaders engage in constructive debate, or is it a "go along to get along" environment? Many a new senior leader has suffered the bitter taste of failure, not because they weren't intelligent or good leaders, but because they didn't take the culture into account.

XEROX'S NEAR COLLAPSE

While there are many examples of the importance of culture, the one that stands out in my mind is the near collapse of Xerox in early 2000. It is a textbook example of the power of organizational culture and how it must be understood, respected, and managed. In 2000, the company reported losses of $384 million on revenue of $18.6 billion.

A March 2001 Bloomberg Businessweek *cover story detailed how new CEO Richard Thoman had gone from hired to fired in thirteen months, due in part to what Thoman described as being "a bad fit."*[8] *Prior to arriving at Xerox as president and COO in 1997, Thoman had had an impressive career serving as CFO of IBM, president of Nabisco, and co-CEO of American Express Travel Related Services. A disciple of*

---

[8] Anthony Bianco and Pamela Moore, "Xerox: The Downfall," *Bloomberg Businessweek*, March 5, 2001, par. 21. http://www.businessweek.com/stories/2001-03-04/xerox-the-downfall

Lou Gerstner, whom he had met at the global management consulting firm McKinsey and followed to American Express, Nabisco, and IBM, Thoman was made CEO of Xerox in April of 1999 but was quickly shown the door. Businessweek *quoted a former Xerox executive: "There was always a huge gap between the visionary aspirations the company nominally was pursuing and what it actually drove employees to do."*[9] *Others blamed the company's misfortunes on the fact that "old-time Xerox employees would not accept newcomers hired to shake up the lethargic Document Company."*[10]

According to the article, Thoman's biggest misstep may have been his push to realign the Xerox sales organization and enter the digital laser printer market. However, those close to the executive ranks agreed that "Thoman, the 'outsider,' never really had a chance to succeed. Xerox was a chummy place; Thoman—a cerebral man not known for his gift of gab—just didn't fit it."[11] *While Xerox has not only survived but thrived under the leadership of "insiders" Anne Mulcahy and Ursula Burns, it has never forgotten the lessons it learned under Thoman. Namely, that every organization has it's unique culture that at a minimum, must be understood prior to implementing new strategies.*

---

[9] Ibid.
[10]
[11]

BEEN THERE, DONE THAT!

To a large degree, I can appreciate the challenges Thoman faced at Xerox. When I became the president of Cub Foods, I felt up to the challenge, even though I had *no* grocery retail experience apart from buying groceries. In my mind, I would come in, roll up my sleeves, learn the business, and then begin to implement. Though I was armed with the best intentions, I neglected the cultural uniqueness of the grocery industry. My tailor-made suits, custom French-cuff shirts, and designer shoes had no place in it. They had served me well in previous jobs, but at Cub they made me seem unapproachable and snobby. It didn't help that I parked my Mercedes S550 next to workers' used Buick LeSabres (the official company car). To add injury to insult, my introverted, reclusive nature made me appear uninterested in the workers who made Cub run.

Less than six months into the role, I was assigned an executive coach who worked with me on being more engaging and visible to associates, more involved with my staff, and more aware of the impact of my presence. I purchased and drove a GMC Terrain instead of my Mercedes, donated my tie collection, and began to dress in a less intimidating way. I dedicated time to being in the stores with my associates and engaging them in helping to create and drive the strategy. The business responded to my efforts to embrace the culture, and eventually it accepted me and my vision for the organization. But without the support of my boss and my team, and my willingness to be flexible, the story might have had a less flattering ending.

FINAL THOUGHTS ON HOW TO EXECUTE AS A CEO

By now, you should be comfortable with the idea that it is OK not to have all the answers. In fact, you might even have breathed a sigh of relief to know that you were not alone in feeling the pressure to have them. However, as a senior leader, you are responsible for the performance of the organization you lead. Here are a few things to keep in mind as you take your leadership journey:

Surround yourself with the "best and brightest" talent you can find. Never forget that you are only as successful as the team you assemble around you. To get the job done and do your best, you will need to hire the best. In fact, don't be afraid to hire those who may be brighter than you are in a given area. As a leader, no one expects you to be the best marketer, technical guru, financial consultant, etc. But they *will* expect the decisions you make in these areas to be well thought out and effective and that you deliver the desired or promised results. To achieve this, you must rely on the collective minds of your team.

And after you hire your team, set the strategy, define the goal, and get out of the way! Innovation and creativity are the lifeblood of any organization. When you consider the success of companies like Apple, Google, GE, IBM, 3M, and others, you can see that their ability to innovate and create new products, services, and markets keeps them leading-edge. To maintain such a competitive edge, these organizations encourage their leaders and associates to be innovative and look for new ways to solve business problems or provide customer solutions. As a leader, you must resist the tendency to tell others how to perform their roles. You must allow them to share their ideas, opinions, and theories in an environment that encourages such. Furthermore, as their leader you must be able to listen, particularly when their ideas don't jibe with your own. To stifle such creativity may cost your company the next iPhone, iPad, Kindle, Post-It Note, or successful Netflix idea.

Understand the key "drivers" of your business, and take personal ownership of decisions in those areas. While it is essential to regulate, mandatory to collaborate, and efficient to delegate, as a leader you must not lose sight of the things that drive the success of your organization. Your board, your boss, your stockholders, your constituents, and even your team will ultimately look to you to take ownership of the organization's performance. And while there may be dozens of daily decisions to make, it's your job to make the call on those that matter most to your business.

REALITY 3

Criticism Will Be More Intense
Get a Thick Skin

By nature, human beings are extremely critical of others. As far back as you can probably remember, someone has always had a negative opinion about something you did or said. I have found in most cases that such critics criticize others for the skills, talents, or ambition that they lack themselves. Years ago, I attended a Celine Dion show in Las Vegas. Celine did a great job and received a standing ovation. Yet, I heard a disgruntled female patron comment, "She was OK, but I thought her outfits were awful!" Now, I would be willing to wager that this woman neither had a voice like Celine's nor a degree in fashion. Yet, like the movie critic who couldn't write a screenplay if his life depended on it, she gets to have her opinion!

Criticism like this only intensifies when you reach the executive ranks. When you accept the role of executive, you become a public figure, of sorts. As such, more people in the organization believe they have a right to evaluate and condemn you for the good of the organization. While some of this mostly likely will be filtered away and never reach your ears, you can and should expect to encounter more negative feedback than in the past. There are several reasons for this:

- **It's easy to be a critic.** It takes no training, effort, or education to become a critic in an organization. You don't have to know the facts, you don't need to understand all of the business intricacies, and you don't even have to be knowledgeable about the subject of your opinion. You are entitled to an opinion regardless of how you arrive at it. As someone once put it, "Opinions are like belly buttons: everybody has one, but what purpose do they serve?"

- **It requires no accountability.** In most organizations, critics have little to no accountability. They can attack ideas, personalities, and even the success of others with virtually no penalty for doing so. Additionally, it actually allows individuals to deflect their own personal accountability, as it allows them to blame their lack of success on "the boss."

- **People need someone to blame.** Whenever things go wrong in life, people need someone to blame. If gas prices are too high, they blame the oil companies. When grocery prices rise, they blame the store owners. And, when benefit costs rise, bonuses get cut, or the company's stock price falls, if you are an executive, they will ultimately blame *you*! In many cases, though, the blame is warranted. When employees suffer due to the weak leadership of the board of directors, the poor decision making of the CEO, and the infighting of company executives, these entities *should* be criticized. Just remember that when you're a leader, the finger of blame will often point your way, justified or not.

- **You are a big target.** As an executive, you have to make decisions daily. Many of your decisions have a direct impact on the business results, compensation, and overall culture of the company. Inevitably, someone or some department or group will find fault with your decisions. Those who engage in such fault finding are not limited to those who work for you—vendors, shareholders, colleagues, and even customers will find you an attractive punching bag.

THE IMPACT OF CRITICISM ON NEW SENIOR EXECUTIVES

Even for the most thick-skinned of us, criticism can be a difficult pill to swallow. It can attack your confidence, quench your self-esteem, and if not understood and managed properly, compromise your leadership effectiveness. Like most who achieve the prized level of executive in an organization, you were probably a great performer, viewed as high-potential with a track record of success. And yet, you may be ill prepared for the increased scrutiny that awaits you. You will be expected to make an impact immediately, drive change, and achieve targets. But in addition, you will have a very short runway and many more observers (and critics) than you are accustomed to.

The reality is, while most organizations have new-hire training, middle management development programs, and various mentoring initiatives, very few offer training to help professionals make the leap from middle management to the executive ranks. Some send new executives to seminars and workshops offered by prestigious universities or even enlist the help of an executive coach. But for most new executives, on-the-job training is all you'll receive.

As a result, many new executives struggle mightily in handling their newfound critics. Some, in fear of being perceived as inflexible, will often undermine their own leadership by changing their position on matters, alternating strategies, and giving in to the fickle whims of their workers. Ironically, these actions ultimately lead to the perception that the leader is "wishy-washy" and has a "flavor-of-the-month" mentality as it pertains to the organization's direction. As a senior leader, people need to know that you make decisions only after careful due diligence and that you stand by your convictions. Only after giving your strategy the appropriate implementation time, and in the face of overwhelming data against it, should you change your position.

HOW A CLOTHING EXECUTIVE LET CRITICISM AFFECT THE BOTTOM LINE

An executive with a leading clothing retailer reacted to dramatic shifts in styles and trends by hiring a new, cutting-edge designer and launching a collection of clothing that was radically different from the brand's former offerings. Even before the merchandise had hit the stores, the executive was criticized for abandoning the company's roots. The relentless criticism got to the executive, and she allowed for the ousting of the new designer.

Clearly, this executive's instincts and fashion sense were correct in hiring the new designer, but she succumbed to peer pressure and criticism and, by not holding to her convictions, ultimately cost her organization significant sales revenue. To make matters worse, she was later criticized even more when a competitor picked up the rejected designer and gained increased revenue at her company's expense.

Those who face heightened criticism for the first time can fall into the trap of taking it personally. Their egos get bruised, feelings get hurt, and they either lash out in anger or isolate themselves from their critics. Either behavior only serves to further impede their effectiveness and growth as executives. If an executive isolates herself, she loses her effectiveness as she ceases to be a voice in the boardroom. Others ultimately perceive her as not being a real player, and eventually her credibility as a leader is questioned. If the executive chooses to become defensive and lash out, she runs the risk of not being viewed as collaborative, or worse, of being seen as a divisive force within the team.

A NEW EXECUTIVE FLAMES OUT FAST

In an effort to drive efficiencies in its supply chain operation, a larger retailer hired Jeff to lead its merchandising unit. A seasoned veteran in the industry, he was hired to "shake things up" and to add discipline and structure to this fairly autonomous and unstructured organization. Sensing criticism and resentment from his new colleagues, Jeff initially tried to be a team player and work better with his new peers. However, it soon became apparent (in his mind, at least) that he wasn't receiving the professional courtesy and respect he deserved. Frustrated by the criticism, Jeff started to make unilateral decisions on matters that needed support from his peer organizations. To his way of thinking, if they didn't want to play with him, they were against him, and he had nothing to lose by bullying them to push through his agenda.

Unfortunately, Jeff's plan backfired: others perceived his actions as self-serving, counterproductive, and disruptive. Ultimately, the CEO and the company's board grew tired of the complaints concerning Jeff's style and behavior, and Jeff agreed to move on after little more than a year in the role.

To be clear, executives are significant organizational investments. As such, care and consideration should be given to protecting the investment. If the organization does not provide adequate support for new executives in terms of executive coaching or mentoring by more senior executives or board members, the individual may never reach his or her full leadership potential, and the organization will not realize the ROI it had anticipated. New executives should be afforded an on-boarding process that not only gives them visibility to the organization's key leaders and business units but provides insight into the organization's cultural norms and behaviors. If, in fact, "culture eats strategy for breakfast," as management consultant Peter Drucker suggests, new executive leaders need to quickly understand the new cultural environment in which they find themselves and best determine how to navigate it.

CRITICISM CAN BE BENEFICIAL

While none of us particularly enjoy receiving criticism, it can prove beneficial. Criticism is a form of feedback. And good, bad, or indifferent, feedback is a gift: it gives you insight into perceptions that may be negatively impacting your leadership effectiveness. I often suggest that executives insist on regular 360(-degree) evaluations. These are anonymous evaluations typically conducted by your organization's talent management team or an outside consultant. Through in-person and online interviews of peers, subordinates, and superiors regarding your areas of strengths and weaknesses, the process provides you with a snapshot of how those with whom you interact see you.

From personal experience, I can tell you that nothing is more encouraging—and discouraging—than receiving 360 evaluation feedback. Usually, the strengths people see in you do not come as surprises. You've been a success because of them. The challenge comes when your perceived weaknesses are called out. In some cases, you will agree that these are areas for improvement, but some feedback will leave you scratching your head and wondering, "What the heck are they talking about?" Very often, negative observations are less in the area of hard skills and more in the realms of your interpersonal skills, decision making, and personality. These types of subjective assessments can cause a great deal of frustration. Additionally, since the feedback is anonymous, you have no idea who among those interviewed perceives you negatively.

A PHARMA EXECUTIVE'S 360 FEEDBACK FRUSTRATION

Each year, a pharmaceutical company provides 360-degree feedback to the executive team. Mark, a newly promoted executive, was surprised to find very blunt commentary from peers and direct reports about his performance and contributions. While the feedback did not seem entirely out of line, it was certainly more criticism than he had received in many years. And since the feedback was anonymous, the executive could not directly address the issues with his critics. As a result, he became overly cautious during meetings, and in an effort to improve the perceptions of him, he tried to be all things to all people. Mark now is very insecure in his role and uncertain about his future with the organization.

While I can relate to Mark's dilemma as to how to deal with anonymous feedback, I firmly believe that such feedback (and criticism) is truly a gift, and if managed correctly, it can actually help an executive enhance his or her leadership style by uncovering blind spots, real or perceived. I see all feedback as fitting into three categories:

- Positive feedback
- Negative feedback that you agree with
- Negative feedback that you don't agree with

Let's take a look at these three types of feedback and how to best leverage all of them to enhance your leadership ability:

POSITIVE FEEDBACK

Of the three, positive feedback is by far the easiest to embrace, since it focuses on areas in which you perform well. Perhaps you are viewed as a people person, a quick study, or a critical thinker. Whatever the skill set, it is something that others perceive you do quite well. Be aware of these positive traits, and make sure to maintain and continue to deploy them as part of your personal brand.

Also, as you gather feedback from various sources, look for commonalities. If several associates perceive you as strong in a given area, it provides confirmation that this is, indeed, one of your strengths. If only a few identify a trait as positive, it may mean that you display it inconsistently and is something you could work to develop.

Last, beware that some positive feedback can have a negative subtext. Recently, a colleague was told that he was "great at office politics." On one hand, it was a compliment, but on the other, the feedback could also be interpreted as saying "You aren't to be trusted. You will do or say anything to get ahead." When you receive positive feedback that could be interpreted as something else, always probe deeper by asking "What does this behavior look like?" Try to ascertain when, where, and how you have demonstrated this behavior in the past. That way, you can best determine if the trait you were complimented for is something you want attached to your brand.

NEGATIVE FEEDBACK THAT YOU AGREE WITH

Though none of us relishes the idea of receiving negative feedback, if we are self-aware, we know we have areas in which we can improve. Sometimes, we were not aware of the criticized behaviors, but after reflection, we agree that the perception is accurate. Such negative traits, behaviors, or shortcomings can derail the career of an otherwise successful executive if not addressed.

A PERSONAL PERSPECTIVE ON NEGATIVE FEEDBACK

As you may imagine, you don't spend over thirty years leading and working with others without receiving some negative feedback, and I am no exception! Some of the negative feedback that I have received (and agreed with) is that I "multitask too often": I can give the impression that I am not interested in what others are saying. The reality is, my mind works in a peculiar way. For whatever reason, I am able to compartmentalize information and activity in such a way that I can listen to a speaker and complete an e-mail at the same time. The problem is, it makes others feel that I don't value them, their time, or what they have to say. After thirty years of working on this, I have improved, but I still I have to make a concerted effort.

As an executive leader, I have also been accused of "not being big on recognition of my direct reports" when they perform well. To be honest, I must admit I need work in this area. As a baby boomer (those born between 1946 and 1964), I grew up with a work ethic that says, "You get paid to do a job." In my old-fashioned way of thinking, if you are only doing what you're paid to do, why should I throw you a parade? The reality is, all *of us (myself included) have an innate need to feel valued and appreciated, particularly when our performance exceeds expectations.*

Over the years, I've learned that while a paycheck is the reward for performing your job, it is not *the biggest motivator in driving performance. I have seen associates raise their performance just to receive a fifty-dollar plaque in front of their peers. I have witnessed sales representatives work until midnight on December 31 to win a trip to Cancun. As incredible as it sounds, I've seen hungry young executives take on extra work not to earn more money but as a "badge of honor" that shows the organization values them. Yes, money is a motivator, but recognition is the best motivator.*

As an executive leader, by learning to receive, acknowledge, and address your less-than-desirable traits or behaviors, you allow people to perceive that you realize you are not perfect and that, even at your level, you are willing to work hard to improve in these areas.

NEGATIVE FEEDBACK THAT
YOU DON'T AGREE WITH

By far, this is the most difficult feedback to receive. Others have called out a behavior, trait, or shortcoming that you adamantly disagree with, even after careful consideration. What do you do? If you ignore the feedback, a negative perception can linger, possibly hampering your effectiveness as a leader. If you are overly defensive, you can appear to be in denial or, worse yet, unconcerned about the impact of your behavior. Or, you can accept the fact that there is a misperception about you within the organization and then put a plan in place to address it.

Whether we like it or not, others' perceptions can become our realities. Sticking one's head into the sand will not make the accusations go away. True leaders recognize, for the good of the organization and their personal effectiveness, that they *must* set aside their pride, ego, and disagreement with the feedback and then work to disprove the perception.

AN INNOCENT REUNION MISINTERPRETED

Horace was a lifelong IBMer who had worked his way up from sales rep to branch manager. For years, he worked hard, exceeded expectations, and performed well in each new assignment. Finally, the day came when he was given the title "trading area general manager," a role in which he oversaw branches in three states.

During visits to the various branches, it was not uncommon for Horace to bump into senior sales executives and managers with whom he had gone through new-hire training years before. These old classmates would meet, hug, and in some cases have dinner after hours with Horace to relive old times. A year into the role, Horace was shocked at feedback given by various individuals that he "favor[ed] longtime IBMers and not those new to the organization."

Confused by the news, Horace asked his human resource VP to investigate further so he could understand why people had this perception of him. The VP found that when newer associates witnessed Horace's behavior with his former classmates, they interpreted it as a slight. They were completely unaware of the old friends' shared training history, assuming wrongly that Horace was simply playing favorites. With this new information, Horace determined that going forward he would hold breakfast meetings with a mix of associates every time he visited a branch. The group would contain newer associates, former classmates, and diversity on every level. As part of these meetings, he would have everyone introduce themselves, share their time of service with the company, and something about themselves that not many people knew. Inevitably, his former classmates would reveal that they had attended early training with Horace and that they were old friends. In time, the negative perception completely disappeared, and Horace was viewed as a down-to-earth, inclusive leader.

HOW *NOT* TO REACT TO CRITICISM

While it is true that criticism can be a good thing, you cannot allow it to dictate and run your life. There are three ways you should *not* react to criticism:

- **Don't let criticism compromise your decisions.** Leaders make decisions, period! The best leaders review the facts, consider the ramifications, understand the risks, and attempt to predict the outcome. Such due diligence cannot be overlooked, but it should not be second-guessed by criticism. Unless there is new information that is vetted and found accurate, you should never allow criticism—or the unpopularity of your decision—to make you compromise it. As a leader, you will *never* be able to satisfy the needs, desires, and agendas of everyone. However, you *will* be held accountable for your decisions—and the results of your decisions.
- **Don't let criticism manipulate your values.** As an executive leader, you must be a person of integrity, vision, and values. This three-legged stool of leadership is so imperative that if any of the three is lacking, your effectiveness will be negatively impacted.

Of the three, your values can be manipulated by criticism, if you allow it to happen. Recently, an executive leader I know was criticized as being too focused on diversity. The complaint focused on her request that every slate of candidates for roles at director level and above contain women and people of color. She was one of the few women in her company's executive ranks and fairly new to the organization herself, and some advised her to soften her stance. But she determined that her personal values insisted on diversity of thought in an organization and believed that it would never be attained without a concerted effort to create an environment that encouraged it. Further, she understood that leadership starts at the top and that she needed to set expectations.

- **Don't let criticism consume your energy.** Some of our most respected leaders have been objects of intense criticism: Abraham Lincoln, Thomas Jefferson, Martin Luther King Jr., Rev. Billy Graham, Hillary Clinton, Mother Theresa, Shirley Chisholm, Indira Gandhi, and coaches like Vince Lombardi. All of them were able to keep criticism from consuming so much of their energy that they were unable to fulfill their purposes. Criticism is not to be ignored; however, it is not to be suffocating either. Address your critics' concerns, weigh them on their merit, adjust as necessary—then move on!

REALITY 4

You're Not Alone, But Sometimes You Will Feel Like You Are
Who's in Your Inner Circle?

W e've heard it said hundreds of times: "It's lonely at the top." For most professionals, it's a phrase that they've heard, but very few will ever be able to test it out because the truth is, most professionals will never reach the top. They will spend the first five to seven years of their careers getting grounded in entry-level roles. After that, they will spend the next ten to fifteen years locked into first-level to mid-level management (think director-level) roles. From there, a select few will rise to the ranks of upper management (VP or senior VP), and the cream of the crop will become executive management (president, executive VP, CEO, chairperson).

While there are challenges at every level in an organization, it is at the executive level that isolation can become a major problem. For the most part, organizations are like pyramids, and the higher you rise, the narrower the environment becomes.

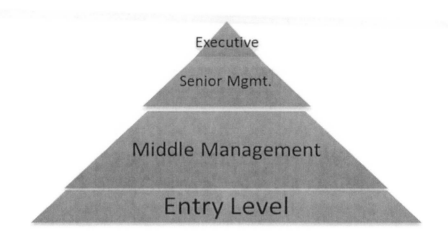

At the executive level, one becomes privy to highly confidential information, such as pending layoffs, possible acquisitions and mergers, pre-announced financial results, key personnel moves, and so on. At the executive level, you are part of the discussion that determines the future of the organization: succession planning, strategic focus, policies, and procedures.

At this level, you are expected to be the public face of the organization with community leaders, government officials, Wall Street analysts, and the dreaded media. One slip of the tongue can send your stock plummeting. One act of indiscretion can make you and your organization tabloid news. Worse yet, strategic errors can take your organization from *Good to Great* to *How the Mighty Fall* (as author Jim Collins put them). In some cases, the pressure of such responsibility can cause a leader to make unilateral decisions, thinking that if "the buck stops [t] here" is true, then he or she needs to make all the decisions and call all of the shots. Many executives develop a sense of paranoia that, if left unchecked, can lead to ineffective leadership and catastrophic results. For this reason, I believe that while it *can* be lonely at the top, it doesn't have to be—nor should it!

FOUR CAUSES OF EXECUTIVE ISOLATION

In observing and coaching executive level leaders in various types of organizations, I have discovered that there are four major causes of isolation. These factors have to be understood and addressed so that an executive leader can be effective in his or her role:

1. **The Need for Discretion**

It is of utmost importance that as an executive leader, you maintain discretion at *all* times. Information is power! The ability to manage information discreetly is leadership. While discretion is important at every level, it is a must-have at the executive level. Given the amount of confidential, top-secret information at your fingertips and your fiduciary responsibility to your organization, lack of discretion for an executive at this level can lead to criminal charges.

BART'S DINNER-TABLE DISCUSSION FIASCO

During a recent Thanksgiving dinner, Bart, a senior executive of a major retail chain, was interrupted by a call on his work cell phone. It was his company's chief legal counsel, confirming that the organization would announce store openings in a new regional market. Unfortunately, Bart took the call within earshot of others at the dinner table. A teenage niece overheard the conversation and immediately shared the information with a high school friend over social media.

The stores were to open under a new name; since Bart had used the code name "Project Patriot" during the call, his niece assumed the new stores would be called "Patriot." Therefore, her message proved harmless. But how exposed might Bart have been if his niece had realized the code name meant that the stores were being planned for the New England area? Could investors and competitors have taken advantage of this information in a way detrimental to Bart's company? Could Bart's own career have been in jeopardy for his lack of discretion?

Given the confidential and sensitive topics to which executives are privy, the number of people with whom they can discuss potentially difficult and complicated matters is limited. As this circle of confidants decreases, a sense of isolation can occur.

2. A Perception of Fairness

Of all the compliments executives can receive about their leadership style, nothing is more appreciated by those under their leadership than fairness. Associates yearn for a leader who treats workers fairly and does not play favorites. Therefore, executives must work hard to avoid perceived unfairness and not appear to have close confidences with select staff members or with members of any specific race, creed, or gender. While there will always be those who by virtue of their roles have more access to the executive than others, it is vital that when decisions have to be made, these individuals are subject to the same rules and regulations as everyone else, consistent with organizational policies.

HONORING NONCOMPETE CLAUSES: A LEADER'S MISSTEP

In many organizations, employment contracts can include a "noncompete" clause. This clause is typically signed by management-level associates and above in exchange for stock options, separation agreements, or other compensation. In essence, in exchange for receiving these perks, an associate agrees not to join, partner with, or create any organization that competes directly with his or her current organization. Most often, these clauses are time bound: they are only in effect for a predetermined amount of time (usually one to two years). If the associate leaves the organization awarding the perks and violates the noncompete clause, he or she is open to litigation from that previous employer.

Claudia, an executive VP at an office equipment manufacturer, learned that one of her protégés had been impacted as part of a recent restructure. The employee was given a severance package, and ninety days later he found a similar position with a lesser competitor. Made aware of this by her human resource VP, Claudia opted not to pursue her former protégé for breaching his noncompete clause. Ironically, another impacted employee with whom Claudio did not have a close relationship with was hired by a larger competitor at a more senior role. Claudia became incensed that this former employee would "join the enemy." She instructed her HR and legal teams to pursue legal action against this "traitor" of the organization. However, during a legal hearing, it was discovered that an exception had been made for Claudia's protégé and that he had been allowed to breach his noncompete. Not only did Claudia's organization have to drop their legal case, they were ordered to pay the legal fees of the other former employee.

3. Filtered Communication

An unwelcome perk executive leaders soon discover is that most of the information they receive is filtered before they receive it. In an effort to please the boss, cover mistakes, or avoid reprimand or reprisal, quite often those closest to the executive make sure that he or she only gets pleasant information. They assume the leader is like the Wicked Witch of the West in the Broadway musical *The Wiz*, who orders, "If you're gonna bring me something, bring me something I can use. But don't nobody bring me no bad news."[12] Likewise, if the leader has an idea that is not so well thought out, most are afraid to tell the emperor that he has no clothes.

Executives in such an environment almost always suffer setbacks, as they are making decisions without the best possible information. The entire organization suffers too, as many brilliant ideas are left on the drawing board or stifled in unpublished PowerPoint presentations that never see the light of day!

JORDAN'S CHALLENGE: THE POWER OF A COURAGEOUS CONVERSATION

I have always been a proponent of sharing as much information as possible with my associates. This is particularly the case when I am new to an organization or leading one in crisis. It has been my experience that in either scenario, if you fail to communicate openly or often, your associates create their own versions of the truth—which usually are nothing of the kind. As president of Cub Foods, I had the challenge

---

[12] King, Mabel. "Don't Nobody Bring Me No Bad News." *The Wiz: Original Soundtrack*, 1978. MCA, 1997. CD.

of communicating with over eight thousand store associates who did not have access to the company's internal communications network. I had the idea of providing updates for my store leaders that they, in turn, could share at weekly "huddles" with their teams.

I felt that I had accomplished my goal (and my senior team agreed)—until the day I was approached by Jordan, a recent college graduate and entry-level employee. He shared with me that although he had access to the company's internal communications network, my message to the troops was either not being conveyed effectively or in some cases not at all. He felt that unless the rank and file could hear my message directly from me and see the passion in my eyes, it would fall on deaf ears.

Working with my communications team, this young man helped create a weekly "YouTube"-like video that could be played in the employee cafeterias. This allowed the entire team to both hear and see my message. After a while, our customer satisfaction scores showed that my relentless focus on providing a "dominant customer experience" was becoming part of the culture. Had this young man not had the nerve to hold such a courageous conversation with me, the business would have not performed at a higher level.

As an executive leader, it's important that you work to receive as much unfiltered information as you can from every level in the organization. The further removed you are from the pulse of the organization, the more difficult it becomes to make sound business decisions.

4. Maintaining Professional Distance

While it is important for executive-level leaders to have their fingers on the pulse of the organization, it's equally as important to guard their reputations and manage perceptions by maintaining a professional distance from those who report to them and who look to them for leadership.

An unfortunate reality of leadership is that people sometimes hold leaders to unrealistic standards. Not that leaders shouldn't be accountable for their actions — but the fact remains that people want their leaders to be as flawless and perfect as possible. That being the case, many executives are reluctant to let others come too close for fear that their imperfections may be revealed. In an effort not to appear weak or incompetent, some leaders isolate themselves from the broader organization. For these leaders, communicating through their direct reports or via well-scripted company letters is the safest way to protect their reputations.

While it has been said that familiarity breeds contempt, I have also found that people will not follow those with whom they have no connection. As an executive leader, it is essential to create "followership." As John C. Maxwell states in *The Power of Leadership*, "Leaders must be close enough to relate to others, but far enough ahead to motivate them."[13] Likewise, Maxwell offers this sage advice in *Be a People Person*: "He that thinketh he leadeth and hath no one following him, is only taking a walk."[14]

---

[13] Maxwell, John. *The Power of Leadership*. Colorado Springs, CO: David C. Cook, 2001. Pg. 12.
[14] Maxwell, John. *Be A People Person: Effective Leadership Through Effective Relationships*. Colorado Springs, CO: David C. Cook, 2007. Pg. 65.

THE CURE FOR ISOLATION

To be an effective executive leader, it is essential that you develop a system of support that keeps you from feeling (and perhaps being) isolated. At some point, every leader needs to vent frustrations, share concerns, express fears, and admit doubts. Furthermore, executive leaders need those who serve under them to feel comfortable enough to share unfiltered information and provide insight into the pulse of the organization. In simple terms, the executive leader can't lead effectively without being surrounded by people—not just *any* people but the *right* people. In *Care of the Soul*, Thomas Moore may have said it best: "We need people in our lives with whom we can be as open as possible. To have real conversations with people may seem like such a simple, obvious suggestion, but it involves courage and risk."[15]

The risk of being vulnerable forces many leaders into isolation. Given the criticism, visibility, and accountability of leaders, it understandably takes a great deal of courage to seek out those with whom you can have a real connection: particularly, peer-level associates who can empathize with your situation. While the task of identifying such individuals is neither simple nor easy, I have found that the most effective leaders identify two sets of support systems: internal and external.

---

[15] Moore, Thomas. *Care of the Soul*. New York: Harper Collins, 1992.

INTERNAL SUPPORT SYSTEMS

The benefits to an executive leader of having internal touch-points far outweigh the pressures of operating in isolation. Internal support systems, comprised of members within the organization, allow you to better understand corporate culture and morale. These systems help you determine if the strategy you've outlined is working or if a midcourse correction is needed. If managed properly, a social media component to an internal support system can yield everything from new revenue opportunities to the sharing of great ideas throughout the organization. While there are many examples of internal support systems, I have both witnessed and benefited from these four:

- **Internal Feedback Mechanisms**

Leaders need to create ways for those in the rank and file to share their ideas, thoughts, concerns, and frustrations. For many associates, just the thought of having a voice in the organization boosts morale. In the olden days, this could be something as simple as a suggestion box. Early in my career, it was not uncommon to see such boxes in cafeteria areas. If so compelled, an employee could share whatever was on his or her mind with the knowledge (or hope) that an executive within the organization would read and respond to it.

Over the years, organizations have become more sophisticated, administering annual or semiannual electronic employee engagement surveys that provide insight into how associates feel about things such as compensation, senior leadership, corporate direction, and job satisfaction. The surveys work to identify potential blind spots an organization may have or work to confirm that employees embrace, identify with, and support the organization's mission and vision.

Taking a more personal approach, many executives like to hold "town hall" meetings or "fireside chats" with associates. They are usually designed to allow a leader to meet with a specific group of employees in an informal setting. The executive often shares an update on the business, but the bulk of the time is spent answering associates' questions.

COFFEE WITH KEITH

I became a huge fan of meeting with associates as an executive within the Bell System, headquartered in Hoffman Estates, Illinois. With my responsibility over a seven-state region, it was very difficult for me not only to develop connections with the various offices but also to appreciate the unique challenges of providing services in each of those markets. To gain a better perspective, I borrowed an idea from a former boss at IBM: I regularly traveled to a specific market and invited associates to meet with me in the cafeteria over coffee and doughnuts.

Later dubbed "Coffee with Keith," these meetings allowed me to get out of my isolated ivory tower and hear firsthand what was on the minds of our associates. Additionally, it allowed me to share the logic and the thinking behind organizational moves and initiatives that they might not have fully appreciated. Over the years, I have made Coffee with Keith a mainstay in my internal support system. It helped me be more connected, effective, and informed than ever before.

While electronic surveys and chats over coffee have proven effective, social media has changed the playing field for internal feedback systems. With the increasing number of Gen X, Gen Y, and millennials in the workforce, many of whom grew up with the Internet, MySpace, and Facebook, it was inevitable that social media tools would find their way into the workplace.

CAN YOU SAY "YAMMER"?

I was introduced to one social media tool by the former CEO of Supervalu, Craig Herkert. In an effort to create a real-time, action-oriented, internal communications system, Mr. Herkert introduced the organization to something called Yammer. Created in 2008 and styled "The Enterprise Social Network," Yammer is a secure, private social network for organizations. Yammer empowers employees to be more productive and successful by enabling them to collaborate easily, make smarter decisions faster, and self-organize into teams to take on any business challenge. Think Facebook for your organization. (In fact, Facebook's founding president, Sean Parker, serves on Yammer's board of directors.)

Yammer allowed store directors from any of Supervalu's grocery chains to post display pictures and to share winning ideas on driving sales and operational best practices. If one store had a great idea on how to drive sales in the deli department, they could take photos, attach a write-up in Microsoft Word, and post it for all other deli managers to see and replicate. Additionally, just as with other social media tools, readers could "like" or "comment" on any post. For the executive leader, it provided real-time feedback and information on what was working and what was not. Now owned by Microsoft, Yammer is used by roughly 80 percent of the Fortune 500.

• Select a First Lieutenant

One of the riskiest but most impactful internal support systems I have ever discovered was the cultivation of what I call a "first lieutenant." Just as Batman needed Robin, just as the Lone Ranger needed Tonto, just as Oprah needed Gayle, as an executive leader, you will need your own first lieutenant to enhance your effectiveness. In my experience, it was extremely helpful to identify that "go-to" member of my leadership team on whom I could rely and ultimately consult with regarding business matters.

Note that I use the words *consult with* and *business*, as opposed to *confide in* and *personal*. Even though you will come to value your lieutenant as a trusted member of your team, I always advise keeping a certain professional distance from those who report to you. On more than one occasion in my career, I've had to break the news to a first lieutenant that his or her department was being downsized or that the job was being eliminated. Delivering such news would have been all the more difficult had the relationship lacked professional distance. However, if managed properly, such relationships can prove invaluable.

It is important that early on you identify members on your team who are positive, proactive, hardworking, intelligent, and discreet. Allow them to prove their worth by having them lead an important initiative or take on a special project. That way, you will gain insight into their business acumen and maturity. Once you are confident that they possess the traits you're looking for, meet with them regularly to get their perspectives on the business, competition, and so on. Additionally, give your lieutenant the right to challenge and question your ideas. This not only creates a sense of inclusion but, in most cases, your end result will be more successful as you gain new insights and perspectives.

Eventually, you will end up with someone you can depend on in a crunch, lean on for ideas, and (equally as important for your lieutenant) sponsor for positions of greater authority in the organization. I have been fortunate enough in my career to have had a few of my first lieutenants grow into peers within the organization. Personally, nothing has been more rewarding than to sit in the boardroom next to a peer you've helped groom.

K. C.'S STORY: "I GOT YOUR BACK, BOSS!"

When I was promoted to president of US operations for Pitney Bowes Management Services, I had not yet worked with any of my new direct reports. I was an outsider from a different division, and several of my direct reports had been unsuccessful candidates for my new position. The job I inherited was a big one—overseeing a dozen football-field size document processing centers; providing business outsource processing for the largest banks, insurers, state agencies, and credit card issuers; and managing the onsite document processing needs of over half of the Fortune 100. It was a daunting task.

However, early on, I observed that one individual showed a great deal of interest in my success. In time, I discovered that what motivated him to take a vested interest in my success was his love for the company and its success. After more careful observation, I determined that K. C. would make an ideal first lieutenant. During our very first meeting over dinner, K. C. stated, "Boss, I will make you two promises. First, I'll never lie to you. Second, I got your back."

Over the years, K. C. and I developed a tremendous working relationship. He would keep me advised of any critical client issues in the business before the molehill could become a mountain, and he kept me abreast of any perception issues I had with associates. I sponsored K. C. for many awards, bonuses, projects, and roles. Years after leaving Pitney, K. C. and I have become good friends, sharing time together with our families and serving as personal references for each other professionally.

• Identify "Field Agents"

As a child, I was amazed at the diversity of my father's friends. At the end of his career as a bank examiner with the Federal Home Loan Bank Board, his friends ranged from banking executives to political leaders, business owners, and pastors. Likewise, he spent time with retired steelworkers and old childhood buddies and would even buy a meal for a homeless person. When I asked about his interesting cadre of colleagues, he shared with me a very important lesson: "Son, it pays to know people on every level."

In my first job after college as a sales rep with Ohio Bell, he encouraged me to be nice to the administrative assistants and to be sure to buy coffee and doughnuts or pizza and beer (hey, it was the early '80s) for the installers of the phone systems I sold. His reasoning was, "At some point, you are going to need one or both of them to cover your behind." In the ensuing years, I realized Dad was right.

As an executive of a large organization in particular, you can't be everywhere at once. But you will be more effective if you have individuals in the field who can provide you with valuable grassroots information. Typically mid-level managers, these "field agents" are your eyes and ears into the real issues within the organization, good or bad. In most cases, these individuals self-select: they ask questions during "town hall" meetings or are assertive enough to e-mail or call your office with issues and concerns. In other cases, they are top performers to whom you, as a leader, should reach out in order to recognize and cultivate a relationship.

With field agents in place, you will at a minimum have another data point with which to make decisions and draw conclusions. During market visits, I sometimes invite my "agents" to dinner to check their pulse on anything from a new compensation plan to new product ideas. The win-win is that you as an executive leader get the benefit of insights deeper within the organization, and the field agents get the benefit of valuable exposure and quality time with a key executive.

- **Keep the Door Open**

This final suggestion is the simplest to understand but can be difficult to execute. In a nutshell, I encourage you not only to have an open-door policy but to actually maintain an open door. Understandably, your crowded schedule means limited access at times, but you should have your assistant pencil in appointments with associates who want them. Unless an associate requests confidentiality, always keep others in his or her chain of command aware of such meetings so you don't give the appearance of letting their subordinates "go over their heads." Likewise, try not to make any solid commitments without all the facts. You will find, though, that your willingness to listen creates a culture of open and honest communications and helps you feel less isolated.

EXTERNAL SUPPORT SYSTEMS

It's also important for an executive leader to have support systems outside of the organization. They are built primarily of peer-level relationships and provide the comfort that comes with spending time and sharing ideas with those who can truly appreciate your challenges. Several executive leaders I spoke with shared that they use the following three external support systems:

- **Board Service**

As an executive leader, you should seek to serve as a director on at least one board of a for-profit or not-for-profit organization. Boards are typically made up of other seasoned, high-level executive leaders who can provide a safe haven to discuss matters that you may not be willing or able to share with someone from your organization. As it can be difficult landing that first for-profit, paid board seat, I suggest you identify a local or national not-for-profit board on which to serve. In addition to the relationships you'll build, you'll gain an appreciation for board governance that will only serve to enhance your leadership skills.

* **Executive Level Professional or Industry Associations**

At every level of my career, I have taken advantage of the networking and development opportunities found in professional and industry associations. Participating in executive-level versions of these associations is just as important when you reach the top.

My involvement with the not-for-profit National Association of Corporate Directors (NACD) helped prepare me for board service in the for-profit arena. Membership in the Executive Leadership Council provided me over three hundred peers with whom I could share ideas, learn from how to negotiate an executive compensation package, and who could provide insight into an unfamiliar industry or private equity opportunity.

HOW THE EXECUTIVE LEADERSHIP COUNCIL HELPS CURTAIL ISOLATION

Created in 1986, The Executive Leadership Council (ELC) is the nation's premier leadership organization comprising the most senior African-American corporate executives in Fortune 500 companies, representing well over 380 major corporations. With more than five hundred members, one-third of them women, the council represents senior executives in positions one to three levels from the chief executive officers of Fortune 500 companies, CEOs themselves, and other entrepreneurs.

Interestingly, it was the death of a member that inspired the ELC to make eliminating executive isolation one of its highest priorities. Years ago, a frustrated, desperate ELC member, overwhelmed with a sense of isolation in her role as an executive leader, took her own life. While outwardly she seemed happy and upbeat, inside, she wrestled with all of the fears, doubts, and insecurities that isolation can bring. In a vow never to have any member experience such isolation ever again, the organization adopted a twenty-four-hour callback policy. In exchange for being selected into the ELC (members must be nominated, interviewed, and meet all membership requirements), you must agree that should you receive an e-mail or phone call from a fellow ELC member, that call must be acknowledged and returned within twenty-four hours. It is the hope of ELC leadership that the organization never loses another member to the perils of isolation.

- **Cultivate Influential Outside Relationships**

Many executive leaders share how they have personally benefited from developing relationships with key influential individuals in the communities in which they do business. From clergyman to community leaders to politicians, there are those who can give you access to their networks and, in some cases, help you drive your business goals.

While serving as president of Cub Foods, my effectiveness was enhanced immensely by two such relationships. At a business conference, I was introduced to Sherman Patterson. The nephew of the late boxing legend Floyd Patterson, Sherman served as a first lieutenant of the then-mayor of Minneapolis, R. T. Rybak. This relationship was extremely helpful in gaining support from the mayor's office on key Cub initiatives, as well as congressional support from Congressman Keith Ellison to help resolve a labor dispute.

Another key external relationship I cultivated in Minneapolis was with Alfred Babington-Johnson and his wife, Anna. One of my major business foci was to have Cub Foods become "the" neighborhood grocer of choice in the Twin Cities area. Being new to the area, I had very few relationships to help drive this initiative. Fiercely active and very well known in the Twin Cities community, Alfred and Anna singlehandedly introduced me to clergy (of all denominations), key business leaders, and the heads of several major community-based organizations. Because of the access they gave me to their network, I was able to reinforce and reestablish Cub Foods as the number one grocery retailer in all of Minnesota.

The best way to avoid isolation as an executive leader is to proactively identify opportunities for engagement. If at all possible, plan town hall meetings, employee engagement surveys, and site visits. If you don't, you will find that your calendar fills up quickly, and you will have little time for such activities. Additionally, identify professional or industry organizations you can join to maintain peer-level networking.

REALITY 5

The Perception Gap Widens
See Yourself How Others See You

No matter who you are or what position you hold in your organization, there are always two perceptions at work. The first is how you see yourself. The other is how those around you see you. Early in your career, the gap between them may be slight. This is primarily because your sphere of influence is relatively small. As a young professional, you are typically an individual contributor and perhaps a member of a small team. Not many people in the organization know of you; you haven't had the opportunity for increased visibility. However, as your role, profile, and position expand, how you see yourself and how others see you can be as different as night and day.

At long last, you are a senior leader, in command of a department, business unit, or other organization. You are an executive director, VP, president, provost, or have some other title of authority. You now manage multiple people, perhaps hundreds or thousands. In your mind, you are a down-to-earth, thoughtful, well-meaning leader. Yet, others view you as stuffy, arrogant, and meanspirited. You consider yourself an inclusive leader with an open-door policy. But those who work under you perceive you as an aloof, standoffish leader who has no time for the "little people."

Without an executive doing anything differently, marked differences develop in how he or she is perceived by others, including those who were recently peers. You will suddenly be treated like a powerful person, even if you don't feel like one. While you will become well known for what you do at work, others will know less about who you are away from the office. Below are some real-life examples that you may find familiar:

- Based on her cost-cutting and no-frills approach to maintaining the budget, the CFO of a large company is widely thought to be cold and dull. In reality, she is a big-hearted friend, a fun-loving spouse, and a generous mother. Most people in the organization don't have access to those aspects of her life; therefore, she must deal with a perception that is decidedly one-dimensional.

- Everyone assumes that the new head of human resources has the power to "make things happen" regarding hiring and compensation decisions, just as her predecessor did. But because of her short tenure and the dynamics of the role, she is not yet able to make unilateral decisions. Since she is assumed to be more powerful than she really is, her staff is disappointed that she is not more deliberate about exerting her will.

- Recently, an organization chose to promote a relatively new hire to an executive role instead of choosing the candidate whom his peers considered more deserving. While the new executive's superior expertise won him the role, his former peers now perceive him as arrogant, cutthroat, and self-serving.

Often, behaviors attributed to executives are not at all consistent with their intentions or with who they are. Being perceived as one dimensional—or worse, as malevolent—can be a very disconcerting experience.

THE SIGNIFICANCE OF PERCEPTION

No matter how much we may dislike it, perception matters. In a world of first impressions, social media sites, such as Facebook and LinkedIn, provide a glimpse into your world (we firmly advocate that leaders greatly limit their use of social media). By the time you are a senior leader, a simple Google search will reveal more information about you than you can imagine (political contributions, salary information, and so on). In many respects, such glimpses make life more difficult for leaders than in days past. We live in a time of twenty-four-hour media, TMZ, CNN, and websites that thrive on sharing the most personal and intimate details of our lives.

As a senior leader, perceptions of you are formed before you ever walk into a room. Perceptions, whether real or imagined, can either enhance or hinder your effectiveness and success. But how and why is perception significant for a leader? Isn't leading just about results? The significance of perception boils down to the following:

- **Perception can help or hurt your ability to create followership among your associates.**

Whether we think so or not, most people are followers. It could be due to fear of failure, insecurity, difficulty making decisions, or a host of other reasons. So, rather than take the "road less traveled" of leadership, they choose to play it safe and let others take the risks.

To be clear, there is nothing wrong with not wanting to be a leader. Leadership and its demands are not for everyone. In fact, to become a great leader, you must first know how to follow. The irony is that most people look for leaders to be not only supermen or women, but also "just like them." And, although most people want a leader they can believe in, they can also be intolerant of their shortcomings (even those they have in common). If others perceive you to feel you are above them or as unable to relate to them, they may choose not to follow you.

PERCEPTIONS AND THE 2012
PRESIDENTIAL ELECTION

A great example of what happens when people perceive someone as unable to relate was the 2012 US presidential election. Republican candidate Mitt Romney should *have been a formidable opponent for President Obama. The economy was still not producing the jobs Americans wanted. Gasoline prices were nearing an all-time high. Foreclosures, unemployment, and bankruptcies were commonplace among the middle class, and President Obama's approval ratings were significantly lower than when he became president. In fact, Romney was so certain of victory that he decided not to even write a concession speech. Unfortunately for Mr. Romney, he had a perception gap that he and his team underestimated and did not do enough to overcome.*

President Obama realized early on that to win the election, he needed to garner the support of Latino, LGBT, elderly, and young voters. To do this, his campaign addressed issues like immigration, gay marriage, social security benefits, and student loans. By speaking to the needs and concerns of these constituents, he was perceived as understanding and supportive. Mr. Romney, on the other hand, was perceived as a super-rich, out-of-touch politician who could not relate to (or couldn't care less about) their concerns. The perception was solidified when a secret campaign video was leaked in which Mr. Romney stated: "There are 47 percent of the people who will vote for the president no matter what. All right,

there are 47 percent who are with him, who are dependent upon govern-
ment, who believe that they are victims, who believe that government has
a responsibility to care for them, who believe that they are entitled to
health care, to food, to housing, to you name it. That's an entitlement. And
the government should give it to them. And they will vote for this president
no matter what. And I mean, the president starts off with 48, 49, 48—he
starts off with a huge number...These are people who pay no income tax.
Forty-seven percent of Americans pay no income tax. So our message of
low taxes doesn't connect. And he'll be out there talking about tax cuts for
the rich. I mean that's what they sell every four years. And so my job is not
to worry about those people—I'll never convince them that they should
take personal responsibility and care for their lives."[16]

Needless to say, this event may have created a tipping point in the
election. By alienating "47 percent" of the population (by which many
perceived Romney to mean poor and middle-class whites, LGBT citi-
zens, and Latinos—but which together actually make up more than 47
percent of the US population), Mr. Romney suffered a crushing defeat
on election night. In a conference call with fund-raisers and campaign
donors, Mr. Romney explained his loss by saying that the president had
followed the "old playbook" of using targeted initiatives to woo specific
interest groups, "especially the African-American community, the His-
panic community, and young people."

---

[16] "Full Transcript of the Mitt Romney Secret Video." *Mother Jones*, September 19, 2012. http://www.motherjones.com/politics/2012/09/full-transcript-mitt-romney-secret-video

While this example is from the realm of politics, the principal message applies to anyone in leadership. If you are perceived as being uncaring, insensitive, out of touch, or lacking in integrity, you are not a true leader. You may have the title, but you won't have the support. In her blog post "The 9 Essential Elements of Leadership," Linda Descano states that leadership is:

1. "Earned by one's actions each and every day, not bestowed by virtue of having the word "manager" in your title"
2. "Being in the service of others, not being served by them"
3. "Humility and integrity, not hubris and self-interest"
4. "Listening more and talking less"
5. "Knowing what questions to ask rather than knowing all the answers"
6. "Connecting ideas, people and resources, not controlling them"
7. "Creating opportunities and removing roadblocks"
8. "Consistency even in chaos and transparency in times of turmoil"
9. "A journey not a destination: it is a process, not an outcome"[17]

If you are perceived as having these traits, your effectiveness and the perception of you as a leader will be enhanced, and you will create followership that supports you even in difficult times.

---

[17] Descano, Linda. "9 Essential Elements of Leadership." *LinkedIn* [blog post], February 20, 2013. https://www.linkedin.com/today/post/article/20130220163206-34334392-9-essential-elements-of-leadership?trk=mp-reader-card

- **Perception has the potential to create allies or enemies among peers and superiors.**

It's no secret that as you move higher up the organizational pyramid, the narrower it becomes. There are fewer roles and fewer promotions, and the competition can become extremely fierce. Years ago, I fell in love with the book *Executive Warfare* by David D'Alessandro. As a battle-tested, straight-shooting former chairman and CEO at John Hancock, David outlined what he calls the "10 Rules of Engagement for Winning Your War for Success." While I have come to understand and embrace many of his rules, two in particular zero in on the importance of managing perceptions and relationships with bosses and peers:

BOSSES: YOU NEED A LICENSE TO CUT HAIR, BUT NOT TO MANAGE AND CONTROL THOUSANDS OF PEOPLE

The relationship you have with your immediate boss is one of the oddest you'll have in life. You generally don't choose this person, you generally don't care for this person, yet you have to honor and obey this person.[18]

---

[18] D'Alessandro, David, and Owens, Michelle. *Executive Warfare: 10 Rules of Engagement for Winning Your War for Success*. New York: McGraw Hill, 2008. http://www.executivewarfare.com/ten-rules/

Bosses: we *all* have them. While it's nice to believe that if you are the CEO or an entrepreneur, you have no boss, such thinking is naïve. If you are the CEO, your boss is the board of directors and, to some extent, the shareholders. If you're an entrepreneur, your boss could be your supplier, banker, and ultimately, your customer. Regardless, even at this level perception is important, because as D'Alessandro contends, "you generally don't get to choose" your boss. Yet, in many ways, you "represent" your boss. Most likely, he or she hired you or was instrumental in getting you the role. Therefore, you are a reflection of his or her ability to recognize and develop talent. Quite often as a senior leader, you may be asked to represent your boss or speak on his or her behalf. At such times, the perception you leave behind can advance, maintain, or derail your career.

A BOARDROOM BUST!

During his boss's two-week vacation in Europe, Richard was asked to represent her at a special senior leaders' meeting. Having helped his boss prepare for such meetings in the past, Richard eagerly accepted and began to prepare himself. Realizing that this was also a moment to gain visibility with his organization's most senior executives, he was determined to create and deliver a stellar presentation.

Normally, each leader would cover the high-level results of his or her business unit, with emphasis on opportunities and risks for the coming quarter. Though typically he would only need to share high-level financials, Richard thought it wise to create a massive presentation with charts, graphs, and detailed financials. While a five- to six-slide presentation was expected, Richard's was twenty. Instead of seeing superiors impressed and fascinated with his detailed presentation, he was greeted with yawns and frowning faces. And, because of the presentation's level of detail, the CEO began to drill down into Richard's numbers and asked questions for which he had no answer.

After vacation, Richard's boss quickly met with him to share feedback from the senior leaders who were at the meeting. Though she called it a "teachable moment" for Richard, he was never again asked to present before the company's senior leaders. Likewise, his boss began to distance herself from Richard, and his career stalled as she stopped recommending him for advancement during succession planning meetings.

Stories such as Richard's happen almost every day. You can enjoy a great relationship and have the trust of your boss. But if some perception of you causes him or her embarrassment and is not addressed quickly, it can negatively impact your effectiveness and advancement within the organization. Remember, you are a "brand," and your brand speaks for you whether you are in the room or not. Understanding any perception gaps with your boss and those superior to you can help you better manage your brand: put plans in place to close any gaps. Further, you never want to be perceived as outshining or upstaging your boss. Your goal should be to make the boss look good: wise for hiring you, great at developing you, and proud to support you. The only thing worse than having your boss be embarrassed by you is for him or her to be resentful of you.

PEERS: UNDERSTAND THAT THEY ARE YOUR MOST VALUABLE ALLIES...OR YOUR MOST DANGEROUS ENEMIES

"It's not important to be the solitary genius who dreamed up, financed, and implemented a great plan all by yourself. What's really valuable is showing that you are the kind of person other powerful people want to work with," write D'Alessandro and Owens.[19]

Perception gaps can be equally problematic with your peers. At this point in your career, you are one of a dozen or so leaders within your organization. Additionally, you and your peers are either being groomed or vetted for roles of greater responsibility. Suddenly, you find yourself under a stronger microscope and being compared with those in your peer group. The difference at this level is, you are not only being measured on your business results; others are taking notice of your ability to influence and persuade your peers and those who don't report to you.

[19] Ibid.

While some of this observation takes place on a personal level (observing you in meetings, projects you lead, and so on), more often than not, a perception of you is molded by the attitudes, comments, and behaviors that your peers have toward you. Early in your career, you were recognized by your ability to get things accomplished on your own. As a senior leader, you will be recognized by your ability to get things done through and with other people.

For most, this is a delicate dance. You want to stand out among your peers, but not in a way that paints you as cutthroat, manipulative, or a glory seeker. Conversely, you don't want to be perceived as lacking in ambition, originality, or ability. You want to stand out, but not to the point of being obnoxious. You want to be viewed as a "go-to" player, but not as someone who never shares the ball. You want to be recognized for your accomplishments without being labeled a braggart. As David D'Alessandro put it, the secret lies in "showing that you are the kind of person other powerful people want to work with."[20]

When relating to your peers, it is important to convey the message: "I'm here to support you so that the *organization* can be successful." Quite often at the senior level, a portion of everyone's compensation is tied to the organization's overall performance. This fact should serve as the common denominator and motivator for driving team success. Individual success, without creating success for the team or organization, never provides the ultimate reward. As great as Michael Jordan was,

---

[20] Ibid.

it was his ability to make those around him better that led the Chicago Bulls to six NBA championships. Be mindful to recognize the successes of your peers. Take time to nurture solid business relationships. And, above all, when it's your time to be recognized, rewarded, or honored, do so with a spirit of humility. Otherwise, you will turn your peers into rivals or, worse yet, enemies.

HOW RECOGNITION AND OVEREXPOSURE ALMOST BACKFIRED

Randal was a newly minted business unit president who had joined the organization from the outside two years prior as a senior VP. Culturally, the company rarely hired senior leaders from the outside. The fact that Randal had been promoted to president after only two years had already raised a few eyebrows within the organization. In addition to his career, Randal was very involved in mentoring programs in his community and throughout the United States. He had written a very successful book, had received several awards for his volunteerism, and was a darling of the media. He had appeared on television, in newspapers, and even on the cover of a popular magazine.

Randal's peers and colleagues were publicly supportive and proud of Randal's accomplishments. Privately, however, they murmured that his outside accolades might give him an unfair advantage, as they were all looking to be the next CEO. Later, their murmuring escalated into secretly questioning if perhaps Randal was spending more time on his outside interests than on those of the organization. In reality, Randal's performance and that of his business unit had not suffered. However, once this perception of Randal became widespread, he had no choice but to limit his outside activities and lower his personal profile.

Perception may set unrealistic expectations that you cannot live up to or elicit behaviors in others that you never intended.

As a leader, you cast a large shadow. You are perceived as someone who is all-powerful and all-knowing and who makes things happen. At the beginning of the chapter, we shared an example of how the perception of a new HR manager was negatively impacted when she was not able to make unilateral decisions, even though her subordinates thought she had that power. Although it was unfair to her, she could not live up to the unrealistic expectations people set for her.

It's also very tempting for leaders to assume a Superman or Superwoman complex, wherein they actually *want* to be perceived as all-knowing, all-powerful, and all-wise. In such cases, they often undermine their own success by placing themselves in a position to overpromise and underdeliver, thus diminishing their effectiveness in the eyes of those around them. Another challenge leaders have with perceptions is that others can easily mistake an action, comment, or suggestion as an order. Therefore, it is essential that leaders be very clear and direct about what is only a suggestion or food for thought as opposed to a direct order.

As the leader, your people want to impress you and make you happy. Just be mindful that sometimes your words may create behaviors you never intended.

RED VELVET CAKE FOR EVERYONE!

I learned firsthand how perceptions and perceived power can elicit behaviors in others that one never intended.

I arrived at Cub after the holiday season and spent a great deal of time in the stores to get a hands-on understanding of what makes grocery stores work. One day, while working in the bakery department, I waxed nostalgic about my love for red velvet cake (and noted that my mother's name happened to be Velvet). Since nobody in the store bakery had ever tasted red velvet cake, I joked that they needed to get the recipe and try it.

Roughly a month later while visiting a completely different store, I noticed that the bakery was full of red velvet everything*! There were red velvet cakes, red velvet cupcakes, red velvet doughnuts, red velvet cookies, and even red velvet doughnut holes! When I asked why the store had such a vast selection of red velvet items, I was shocked at the answer I received from the bakery manager: "Because* you *said we had to carry it!"*

Never in my wildest dreams had I thought a simple comment from me would drive such behavior. But because of my role as president of

Cub Foods and the perception of power that came with it, my team mistook my love of red velvet cake for a mandate to place it on the shelves.

The story did have a happy ending, however. When we gave out free samples to acquaint shoppers with red velvet cake, it became one of our best holiday sellers!

HOW DO PERCEPTIONS BECOME DISTORTED?

In my experience, no one sets out to create a distorted view of him- or herself. Most leaders have a sense of the persona they would like others to perceive and generally work to display positive traits that provide an atmosphere of inclusion, innovation, and integrity. With such honorable intentions, many leaders are disturbed to learn that those who work with them, for them, and around them perceive them in ways they neither recognize nor understand. While the reasons for distortion can be many, the following seem to be the major contributors:

- Lack of Self-Awareness

I'm often surprised at the number of senior leaders who have major blind spots about their habits, quirks, and idiosyncrasies that cause others to see them in a less than positive light. The *Oxford English Dictionary* defines "self-awareness" as: "conscious knowledge of one's own character, feelings, motives, and desires." Anthony K. Tjan, co-author of the *New York Times* Bestseller *Heart, Smarts, Guts, and Luck*, observed in his own experience and research that this reflective trait stands alone as the *one* quality that makes successful leaders:

The best thing leaders can do to improve their effectiveness is to become more aware of what motivates them and their decision-making. Without self-awareness, you cannot understand your strengths and weakness, your "super powers" versus your "kryptonite." It is self-awareness that allows the best business-builders to walk the tightrope of leadership: projecting conviction while simultaneously remaining humble enough to be open to new ideas and opposing opinions. The conviction (and yes, often ego) that founders and CEOs need for their vision makes them less than optimally wired for embracing vulnerabilities or leading with humility. All this makes self-awareness that much more essential.[21]

Though well-meaning, many leaders lack the self-awareness required to leverage the best out of themselves or the organization. For many, the journey to self-awareness begins with emotional intelligence. Though an often misunderstood term, educational psychologist Kendra Cherry's article "What Is Emotional Intelligence?" explains:

---

[21] Tjan, Anthony. "How Leaders Become Self-Aware." *Harvard Business Review Blog Network,* July 19, 2012. http://blogs.hbr.org/tjan/2012/07/how-leaders-become-self-aware.html.

Since 1990, Peter Salovey and John D. Mayer have been the leading researchers on emotional intelligence. In their influential article "Emotional Intelligence," they defined emotional intelligence as, "the subset of social intelligence that involves the ability to monitor one's own and others' feelings and emotions, to discriminate among them and to use this information to guide one's thinking and actions (1990).[22]

Cherry describes the "four branches of emotional intelligence" proposed by Salovey and Mayer as:

1. **Perceiving Emotions.** The first step in understanding emotions is to accurately perceive them. In many cases, this might involve understanding nonverbal signals, such as body language and facial expressions.

2. **Reasoning with Emotions.** The next step involves using emotions to promote thinking and cognitive activity. Emotions help prioritize what we pay attention and react to; we respond emotionally to things that garner our attention.

3. **Understanding Emotions.** The emotions that we perceive can carry a wide variety of meanings. If someone is expressing angry emotions, the observer must interpret the cause of the anger and what it might mean. For example, if your boss is acting angry,

---

[22] Cherry, Kendra. "What is Emotional Intelligence." *About.com Psychology*, November 22, 2012. http://psychology.about.com/od/personalitydevelopment/a/emotionalintell.htm.

it might mean that he or she is dissatisfied with your work, or it could be because he got a speeding ticket on his way to work that morning or that he's been fighting with his wife.

4. **Managing Emotions.** The ability to manage emotions effectively is a key part of emotional intelligence. Regulating emotions, responding appropriately, and responding to the emotions of others are all important aspects of emotional management.[23]

• Lack of Connection

As a leader, never forget that it's about the *people*! Of all the assets on your balance sheet, none is more valuable than your human capital. Nothing gets done without people, and they will worker harder and perform better for a leader with whom they feel a connection. It's not that they want to know the details of your personal life or how much money you make. They aren't overly concerned or impressed with how brilliant you are. But they *do* want to know that you are a "real" person and that you value them as people and the work they do.

Too often as leaders, we neglect to make time and find ways to interact with our people. There always seems to be another meeting, conference call, or closed-door session on the calendar. But when you neglect to find ways to connect with your people, you leave them no

---

[23] Cherry, Kendra. "What is Emotional Intelligence." *About.com Psychology*, November 22, 2012. http://psychology.about.com/od/personalitydevelopment/a/emotionalintell.htm

other choice than to create an image in their minds of who you are. Typically, they end up viewing you in a much more negative light and carry a false perception about who you are.

• Lack of Concern

Sadly, some leaders don't feel it necessary to understand and manage perceptions of them. They are aware of the gaps but make no effort to bridge them. Crippled by an unhealthy sense of ego, these leaders don't grasp the importance of connection, communication, and perception on their effectiveness to lead an organization. While some prove to be successful in spite of themselves, more often than not, such leaders fail to move the organization forward. And those who do often leave the organization worse off than they found it.

HOW TO MINIMIZE PERCEPTION GAPS

Communicate and connect. Early and often, look for ways to connect with those around you. Share a glimpse of who you are away from work. Provide insight into your personal values and beliefs. And be willing to be transparent about your goals for the organization. You could try the popular, informal "town hall" meeting method we've mentioned, where a leader can share business goals and objectives while simultaneously providing insight as to who he or she is as a person.

Display a willingness to help. As a leader, you must never be unwilling to roll up your sleeves and help "change a tire" if need be. Not only should you be willing to change your own tires, you should be up for helping peers and colleagues to change theirs as well. In doing so, you demonstrate a humility that those you lead admire and that those you work with appreciate.

Be aware. Understand that feedback is a gift. Be aware of your brand, image, and perceptions. Take advantage of 360 feedback, employee engagement surveys, and other tools of self-awareness. Once you are enlightened, you can be aware. Once aware, you can minimize the gap between who you are and how others perceive you to be.

Part II

Managing the Personal Challenges That Come with Leadership (from a Coach's Perspective)

REALITY 6

Your Values Will Be Put to the Test
Being Yourself versus Being a Leader

We all have values that guide our lives and determine what we think, what we do, and how we feel. Most people are calmer and feel more like themselves when they can be true to their values. If you value telling the truth—even in the most difficult situations—then you are not very likely to lie and will feel uncomfortable and disappointed in yourself if you do. You will seek out and remain friends with others who value the truth and avoid those who don't. Also, you will avoid putting yourself in situations where you cannot tell the truth. Our values are powerful because they predict our behavior not only when we are being observed but, most important, when no one is watching, as the following story illustrates:

Alicia had recently been promoted to the role of vice president of marketing for Vortex, a human resources software development company— but she wondered if an executive level role was the right fit for her. As someone who had grown up in the company and recently celebrated her twelfth anniversary there, she had finally entered the executive ranks. When Alicia joined the company, she was impressed by how open and "real" everyone was. In the early days, she and her colleagues would work together for long hours, including weekends, to get products to market quickly. As a result, a camaraderie developed between them based on respect, generosity, and shared goals. They often described themselves as a family.

Through the years (and several acquisitions), the company had grown and was now a leader in its field. In the past year alone, Vortex had acquired two other companies. Alicia had been promoted many times, sometimes before she was even ready or prepared for her new responsibilities. But Alicia stepped up to each of the challenges and grew nicely into her jobs. Lately, the economic landscape for Vortex had become more competitive, and clients began to demand new, integrated products and services. In addition, Vortex's employee population had doubled several times over. While there were still some remnants of the early culture, the work environment was becoming quite different.

Alicia had been a committed and loyal employee, with values similar to the company's. One of the core values that she shared with the organization was honesty with colleagues, even when it's hard. During a regularly scheduled meeting with her boss, Sean, Alicia was told that the company would be reorganized within the next six months and redundant jobs eliminated. Specifically, Alicia would lose 20 percent of her staff, since each acquisition already had its own marketing department. Sean showed Alicia a spreadsheet that indicated who would be eliminated, demoted, or get a salary adjustment. He told Alicia that she could not talk to anyone about the reorganization until she was directed to do so.

Alicia knew in that instant that times really had changed and that there would be consequences of the company's growth that she'd never really thought about before. If a decision this big had been on the table in earlier days, she would have been a part of the discussion. She had to put her personal feelings aside, though, because some of the people she worked closest with and considered dear friends would be negatively impacted by the reorganization.

Alicia was not surprised when Mark, her director of marketing for the northeast region, approached her one evening as she was leaving the office. He told her that he had heard about the reorganization and asked if she knew anything about it. He also wanted to know what impact it would have on him personally. Mark was a good performer who had been with Vortex since the beginning. Even though Mark was smart, reliable, and dependable, he was viewed as kind of old-fashioned and reluctant to change. He was a perfectionist and was slow to achieve results. He sometimes missed opportunities to improve performance. Alicia knew that Mark was on the list of individuals who would be asked to leave. When he approached her directly that evening, Alicia told Mark that she did not have any information regarding the reorganization. She told him that if she became aware of any plans for it, she would let him know.

Immediately after their conversation, Alicia felt like a traitor in a way that she never had before in her entire career. In the days that followed, she became more uncomfortable and stressed and had a terrible time sleeping. She knew in her heart that she had not been honest with Mark, and she began to avoid him to minimize her stress. Of course, this made Mark more suspicious and anxious, which was ultimately reflected in a further decline in his performance.

As her executive coach, I knew that Alicia's personal values were being tested. She felt that, as a colleague and friend, she owed Mark the truth. But as a leader in the organization, it was her responsibility to help minimize the disruption that can often come from reorganizations by adhering to the company's communication strategy. After a while, she became angry at herself and her organization for putting her in such an awkward position where she was forced to choose. She was experiencing what many executives do: a conflict between personal values and company values.

HOW VALUES CHALLENGES ARE DIFFERENT AT THE EXECUTIVE LEVEL

How senior leaders in positions of authority navigate their way through the values maze has a profound impact on the rest of the organization and the individuals working in it. While we know that every professional, regardless of level or functional responsibility, has a set of values that has the potential to be challenged at some point or another in the work environment, there are several reasons why the dynamic surrounding values is particularly loaded for more senior-level leaders.

- **Their positive values shape the values of others.** Given their influence, executives and senior leaders have an amazing opportunity to shape the values of others. The impact of good executive-level behavior can be astounding. The decisions an executive makes, particularly under challenging circumstances, send a clear message about what is acceptable, what is valued, and what is frowned upon. This level of impact both directly and indirectly affects the organization's ability to do great things, such as attract and retain top talent, create stand-out products and services, and so on.

- **Their mistakes have greater impact.** Executive-level mistakes can influence the organization's culture and other people's values in a profound way as well. At Enron, for example, while there is no question that a multitude of factors contributed to the demise of the company (and many others since then), a significant part of the dynamic had to do with the culture that senior leadership created through their values. Their choices and the behaviors they exhibited when times got tough sent a signal to the leaders below them about acceptable business practices.

- **Their values are long lasting and can influence company culture.** Decisions that executives make can have lingering effects in the organization for years to come. Steve Jobs, co-founder of Apple, is gone, but his vision and life's work will linger on in his organization and influence the products, services, and impact it continues to have all over the world.

- **Their enormous positional power is influenced by their values.** Executives can set policy that influences many people to support the direction they feel is right for the organization. For example, customer service, human resources, and investment policies can shape the success of any organization. Executives can create new markets, products, and services that don't yet exist, and they often use the conviction of their beliefs and values to convince others to support their efforts. Even if they don't get a large groundswell of support, an executive can still make the call to move ahead with an initiative. It's risky, and there's a lot of pressure on the senior leader, so, hopefully, strong personal values will help him or her to make the right call.

- **Executives live under intense scrutiny.** Often, an executive is under the scrutiny of regulators, governance committees, politicians, and community advocates. The higher an executive is in the organization, the more impact these stakeholders have on his or her life. An executive's actions have great consequences, both negative and positive—and as such, they demand greater oversight. The spotlight is on the choices he or she makes, both personally and professionally, and how those ultimately impact the organization's bottom line.

HOW COMPANY VALUES FIT INTO THE PICTURE

Not just individuals have values; companies have them too. A company's values are often found framed on its walls, helping to let employees, customers, stakeholders, and other constituencies know how they can expect the company to behave as it conducts business. Company values suggest to employees how they will be treated and how they are expected to treat each other. They also determine how employees should behave when building relationships and tell them what they need to consider when making business decisions.

As an executive, your personal values may at some point conflict with those your organization espouses. Usually, such conflicts are small and can be resolved by using good judgment. However, they can sometimes be so critical that you may have to consider more significant measures to resolve them—including reassessing whether the organization is the right fit for you and possibly choosing to depart. Your values will be tested if you are expected to engage in behavior or make decisions that force you to choose between what you think you ought to do and what the company wants you to do. When this happens, it can make you feel stressed and uncomfortable in a way that can deeply impact your performance and your commitment to the organization.

COMPANIES HAVE SPOKEN AND UNSPOKEN VALUES

Most companies have a set of core values that are documented for all to see. You can find them in brochures that go out to customers, framed on the walls at headquarters, or posted on the company website. These statements often describe what the company strives to be like. Typical values might include respect for employees, respect for customers, innovation, integrity, doing the right thing in the face of adversity, rewarding employees for their contributions, compassion for others, and so on. Employees find such values embedded in many of the company's processes and systems, such as recruitment and development. Employees may also find themselves evaluated on company values during performance management reviews. The underlying message is that with a clear set of corporate values, the company can communicate what it stands for, how it will meet its goals and objectives, and how it provides shareholder value. An organization should stand for something, and its values are a good way of articulating what that is. Unfortunately, though companies often articulate what they say they value, it is not always translated into behavior that aligns with it.

Companies, like people, don't always behave in ways that reflect their stated values. For instance, a company may say it values work-life balance, yet employees who try to take advantage of this value may in fact find that they are overlooked for promotional opportunities. In other words, they quickly realize that the *actual* (and unspoken) value is closer to "You can keep your job while maintaining work-life balance, but you can't advance to the higher levels of the organization unless you put the job first."

A less intense example of an unspoken organizational value might be one that Keith mentioned in an earlier chapter: "Your fancy, expensive car means you're just not one of us." Some companies believe that the display of status in cars, clothes, and jewelry is distasteful and undermines the egalitarianism they want to project. Unspoken company values suggest that if you are a wealthy senior executive, it is not in good taste for you to openly display it, because it rattles employees who earn a lot less than you do.

Unspoken values are part of the glue that holds organizations together. Like the best glue, though, they do this without being visible. It is ironic that unspoken values may be the most important yet the most difficult to figure out. Here are some tips to help you uncover your company's unspoken values:

- **Find a mentor.** Take the time to build a relationship with a mentor or someone in your organization who is aware of the firm's subtler unspoken norms and values and is willing to share them with you. People who have been around for some time have seen how values are demonstrated, rewarded, or reprimanded in the organization. This means that it is critically important to ensure that your relationship network is broad and deep—and that you have strong relationships with people who can help you understand the history and dynamics at play. Knowing the unspoken values can be as important to your success as knowing the spoken ones. Recognize, though, that the employee who shares the unspoken values takes some risk here, since often the values are not ones that the company wants to talk about or address openly and publicly.

- **Watch what other people do.** Finding unspoken values often requires you to have good instincts and insights into people and organizational dynamics. When I introduce this subject to new executives I'm coaching, they often ask, "If the values are unspoken, how do I know what they are?" It's not as difficult to uncover them as it may seem. If you don't have a mentor to fill you in, learn to trust your gut feelings, and watch others closely, with special attention to the subtle nuances of their behavior (in addition to the most obvious ones). For example, your company may have a stated value of respect for individuals, including a restriction on using foul language. You notice that no one ever uses foul language in meetings, yet it is often used in private conversations. Even if your boss uses a few choice curse words when he or she becomes heated, don't assume that it is OK to use such language freely. Another place to watch for spoken versus unspoken values is in meetings. Listen to what other executives say while conducting meetings or giving presentations. Notice also *how* they say it, as well as what they are *not* saying. Think more about the tone and feel of situations when executives interact in the organization. Mimic their behaviors and tone.

- **Ask for feedback.** If you give a presentation whose content you feel is good, but you just don't have a good feeling about it when you leave the room (the audience is quiet, no one asks questions), chances are that you've done or said something a bit off base. Ask someone from the audience for feedback. Even if you feel it's risky to ask others because it might show you have a blind spot, take the risk and ask anyway. Keep in mind that if you *feel* like you did something inappropriate, you're probably right. Learn to trust your instincts and intuition. Once developed, they will usually lead you in the right direction about which norms and values should guide you in future, similar situations.

YOUR PERSONAL VALUES: WHAT YOU BELIEVE DETERMINES WHO YOU ARE

Most of us probably don't think much about our values at all until we feel we have to compromise one of them. But you probably have values that affect the kinds of relationships you have with others, how you get your work done, how you handle a crisis, and so on. Personal work values can include honesty, integrity, collaboration, generosity, performance recognition, flexibility, autonomy, and the like. Clearly, all individuals in an organization do not always share the same values. For example, you may value collaboration, feel that it's important to share information with others, and believe that others should do the same with you. Yet, a colleague may believe that sharing information might put him or her at a competitive disadvantage and therefore keep everything close to the vest. The question then becomes whether you should continue to share your work and feel uncomfortable because others don't reciprocate, or not honor your value for collaboration and begin to keep information to yourself that you would otherwise share. Either way, the issue will need to be resolved so that it doesn't distract you from achieving results.

Altering a value you believe in can be very difficult. Your work values have a lot to do with how you become a leader in your organization and the successes and failures you have in the future. These values don't necessarily determine what you do but, rather, how you approach things and what you consider when you are faced with decisions. You must know the values that are important to you so that you can go after the right career opportunities, avoid value-laden conflicts when you are on the job, and associate with the kinds of people and situations that work best for you personally. In short, you must determine your core values.

HOW TO DETERMINE YOUR CORE VALUES

To determine your core values, ask yourself the following questions. The answers will provide you with a good idea of your work values.

1. What would make you extremely happy on your job?
2. What would make you feel most secure on your job?
3. What would make you trust your company?
4. What would make you quit your job?

When Alicia, whom we met earlier, was faced with whether or not she should tell her colleague Mark about the company's reorganization, she asked me, as her coach, to help her decide. I suggested that it might be a good time for her to review her core values.

She knew that she would quit her job if her company did not operate with integrity and if her bosses were not honest with her. In addition, she would not feel good about where she worked if she wasn't respected and able to work collaboratively on projects that challenged her. She would not be happy in a company where she was not rewarded for her contributions, and she would have real trouble with a boss who looked over her shoulder all the time. She recognized that she would feel most secure in an organization that treated others fairly, developing appropriate policies and procedures and applying them equitably. From here, we determined that Alicia's core values included respect for individuals, integrity, teamwork, performance-based recognition, fairness, and independence.

If you should find yourself in a situation like Alicia's, take the time to really think through each of the questions above and determine the values associated with your answers.

KNOW YOUR DEAL BREAKERS

Knowing your core values is only part of the challenge. You must also know which values are your "deal breakers," because these will cause you the most difficulty if you compromise them. A deal breaker is a breach of values that an executive cannot overlook and ultimately outweighs any redeeming qualities of a job. Alicia did not know if having to lie to her direct report and friend was a deal-breaker value. She knew that she felt angst about having to conduct herself that way, but she didn't know what to do about it.

You should know your deal breakers! Knowing them will help you to make better and more efficient choices while minimizing organizational drama. Take the short quiz below when trying to determine if a value is a deal breaker. If you answer yes to any of these questions, then it is likely that you're wrestling with a deal breaker.

Is This a Deal Breaker?

1. Do you believe that the actions required of you are illegal or shady?

2. Are you unable to tell anyone—not even your closest friend—about your action?

3. Will you, for the foreseeable future, feel like a smaller person if you do this?

4. Do you believe that you could get fired for cause because of this action?

5. Will you be able to forgive yourself for this action, or will you feel guilty all the time?

6. Could what you need to do damage your reputation permanently?

As soon as you believe that there is a fundamental difference between the company's values and your deal-breaker values, you should begin your exit strategy. As frustrated as you may be with the senior leaders and the organization's policies, they are probably equally frustrated with you. Your bosses have the power in this situation; they can decide to terminate you at will, and it may come as a surprise. Take accountability for what you believe in. Don't sulk and complain and hope that things will get better, because that is not likely to happen. Take the high road and see things for what they are. We can't expect to fit in to every type of organizational setting. By seeing such situations for what they are, you create more options for yourself.

HOW TO ADAPT YOUR VALUES WHEN THEY CONFLICT WITH THE VALUES OF OTHERS

It is easy to understand how an executive can become lulled into a false sense of security about how much power and control he or she has. Don't be surprised at how hard it actually is to galvanize others to help you achieve your goals if your values and those you lead or work with differ. You may feel that it is your way or the highway and fully expect others to understand that you are, after all, in charge…of at least of part of the organization. The truth is that you are under intense scrutiny. You're expected to make things better and get results. And to get them, you will be required to be flexible in your approach and perhaps adjust your values a bit in the process. For you to succeed, your values must align somewhat with those of the company. No matter the size or scope of the job, understand that you will never be exempt from the need to think carefully about what you value and how it impacts the organization's people and their ability to get things done.

So what do you do when your values are in conflict with others and are essentially being put to the test? Signs that this may be happening include a nagging feeling you cannot ignore, literally losing sleep over some request that just doesn't sit right with you, and knowing that other professionals or friends you respect would never make the choice you feel you have to. Most important, you may simply feel that compromising or adjusting your value will make you feel inauthentic or dishonest. If you asked your deal breaker questions about the situation, you'd probably get similar answers. The signs you're getting probably cause you to feel very uncomfortable—yet they must be addressed, and you must take action.

Even when you know both your core and deal-breaker values, situations that involve your values are frequently complex and cloudy. Quite often, you (and the organization) are actually best served by modifying or adjusting your values in some way. Suppose that you value working independently, without responsibility for team results—but you see that most company projects involve cross-division cooperation. You might try working with a team on a project to experience the results that emerge when different points of view are incorporated in a project or decision making process. As a result, you could add to your beliefs and adopt a new value regarding teamwork.

You must make a judgment call on what to do when your values and those of the company conflict. If the value you're being asked to adjust is a deal breaker, you might have to consider—well—breaking the deal. An example might be integrity. If you were a doctor and believed that you should only suggest surgical procedures as a last resort, you could not work effectively in a practice that recommended surgery just because it provided more income. You would lose respect for your colleagues in the practice (but most important, for yourself). Some values simply should not be compromised, and only you know which ones they are. However, some values you might simply need to be a bit more flexible about—for your own good and for the good of the company. Knowing the difference comes with seasoning, experience, and professional maturity.

So how do you adapt your values when they conflict with the values of others? Here are a few suggestions to consider that can get you on the right track.

1. **Reframe your values.** Modifying a value suggests that it is still important to you; it just had to be reframed to help ensure that you grow and become a successful professional. For example, you may value honesty and transparency in your friendships, and that can and should remain important to you. But in a work environment, certain information you will not be able to share, even with people you consider close friends. You still value friendship, but the way that value is exhibited at work has to change. As an executive coach, I am often given "inside" information about

companies with whom I work. Once, I was told that Jerry, a client and friend, was going to be moved to a different department. Even though I knew that he would appreciate that information, it was not mine to share. This situation flew directly in the face of my value for authenticity. So, how did I remain authentic? By making sure that Jerry understood the rules of engagement for working together at the onset of our coaching relationship. I told him ahead of time that I might know things that I could not share and that this was typical in executive coaching processes. I was able to maintain my value of authenticity by providing rules that Jerry and I could both live by regarding the sharing of information. When Jerry was finally told that he was being moved to a new job, he assumed that if I had known, I was not at liberty to say.

2. **Give it time.** It is important to recognize that modifying a value doesn't often happen overnight. Suppose, once again, that you place a high value on working independently, but you have been asked to be a part of a team that practices a very collaborative style of problem solving. You may abhor others telling you what to do or looking over your shoulder. To you, independence means that you are given your instructions and then are not bothered until you complete your assignment. You want the autonomy to decide how to get your work accomplished. How long do you think it would take you to get used to working with people who

value collaboration more than independence? As you can imagine, it would not be as easy as flipping a simple switch to modify your value. You first need to commit to making the adjustment and then to have many experiences where you can try out the modified value and feel the outcome. This requires patience and commitment. At the end of the day, you might find that while you still value your independence, you are now more open to a more team-based approach to problem solving.

3. **Demonstrate Good Judgment, and Compromise.** Sometimes a conflict arises between people who both have positive—but different—values. For example, some vegetarians don't eat meat because they see it as cruelty to animals. Other people do eat meat, because they like it and believe that the body is healthier when it absorbs animal protein. Neither of these values is inherently right or wrong. The question is, how do they coexist in the real world? As a mature professional, you need to know when a value must be compromised, and you must be willing to accept the consequences with a positive attitude. You may find yourself in a meeting or as part of a team that needs to make decisions for the greater good of the organization.

Imagine two executives in a fashion company—the head of sales and the head of marketing. Celeste, the VP of sales, values consistency, dependability, and commitment to what customers want. She believes that "you don't mess with a formula that works." Eric, the VP of marketing, has different ideas. He values innovation and creativity and believes that success means "staying ahead of the curve"; otherwise, you'll be "left behind on the fashion fringes." In a nutshell, Eric values innovation and forward thinking, while Celeste values commitment and tradition. None of these values are wrong. However, they are different enough to stall progress toward the VPs' common goal of improving shareholder value. If Celeste cannot see the value of innovation and forward thinking, her company will likely remain a follower in the industry and miss key opportunities to innovate as her customers change. On the other hand, Eric enjoys the excitement and unpredictability that comes with doing new things, but if he goes too far, he will drive away his customer base. Good judgment and compromise are required for these leaders to meet in the middle and jointly move things forward—to be flexible enough to achieve success in both the short and long term—and to do it with a positive attitude.

WISDOM AND VALUES

Before you're even hired, you can learn a lot about the values of an organization, department, team, or group by asking the right questions and getting references about organizations, just as they gather references about you. If you find that your values conflict with most of your current organization's values or the values of the people with whom you associate, then perhaps you were not selective enough, and you may need to strategize about how to move on.

Most companies have stated values. If they are not obvious on the company's website, ask to see them during the interview process. Also, search the web (with appropriate caution, of course) to find out what previous employees have said about working at the organization you are considering. Just be careful not to let "sour grapes" information stop you from looking for more balanced opinions and perspectives. Ask other professionals you know if they have any information about the organization. And when you are interviewing for new jobs, never trash your previous company for its values. Instead, talk about the values that are important to you and ask whether you are likely to fit well into the new organization.

Executive life will require much from you. Those who work for you will expect you to have the wisdom and insight to do the right thing, even when it is complicated and challenging. Even in the most difficult of situations, you can find a solution that fits the needs of as many stakeholders as possible while maintaining a clear focus on company goals. This means that you will have to find solutions to novel problems and adjust your values in ways you may not have considered before.

The wisest decision, though, may not be the one you personally prefer or suit your wish to have things go your way. You must always challenge yourself to identify the solution that will best benefit the whole, both in the short and long term. At times, you may believe that adjusting your values can only lead to a bigger problem for your team or organization, but you might just need to look at the situation from another angle. For example, a high-powered executive once asked if he was supposed to compromise his high standards to keep his employees happy. Obviously not! He could learn to value other things, though, such as simply meeting an objective rather than insisting on exceeding it. That way, he could still achieve good results while not overworking employees who valued their free time. Sometimes, being flexible and giving in a little helps you help others become more flexible about adjusting their own values.

In the final analysis, neither your values nor the ones that your organization runs by are to be taken lightly. It is true that your values will be tested. However, in most situations, you can find a way to adjust your values to do what is best for the whole organization. Your values will keep you in good stead as a person and as an executive and will allow you to serve as a role model for those you lead.

REALITY 7

Embrace Constructive Conflict
Driving Innovation, Creativity, and Results

Often, leaders who are driven to achieve results believe that conflict and discord within their teams or among employees hinder progress. They believe that a culture that encourages and preserves harmony is the standard by which team and employee dynamics should be judged. Therefore, employees are discouraged from asking any question that stops the action and causes others to think. Employees are seen as uncooperative when they disagree with standard practices or people in positions of power, influence, or expertise.

Conflict-averse cultures create what we call the "conflict void," where ideas are suppressed, employees are demotivated, and potential goes unrealized. This is not to suggest that leaders should create conflict for its own sake but, rather, that they should encourage constructive conflict that challenges the business and employees to get the very best results.

As Robert Towsend said, "a good manager doesn't try to eliminate conflict; he tries to keep it from wasting the energies of his people. If you're the boss and your people fight you openly when they think that you are wrong—that's healthy." Constructive conflict is necessary to consistently achieve exceptional results for the following reasons:

- It challenges the organization to find new solutions to old and existing problems
- It helps employees to develop deeper thinking skills
- It helps the organization to find ways to innovate and create
- It helps individuals to become more comfortable with receiving feedback and having ideas challenged
- It allows disagreements through which can come new insights about what is being done and why

THE CONFLICT VOID

A conflict void occurs when conflict is not allowed to exist or when it is not managed. Both will damage relationships and hinder a team's success.

There is a conflict void when:

1. Harmony is encouraged over lively debate and dissenting opinions
2. Individuals are afraid to offer differing opinions for fear of reprisal
3. Fear of expressing emotion prevents individuals from providing important and essential information
4. Emotions and passions are not managed in a mature way

Conflict voids occur under several communication cultures:

- **Don't ask, don't tell.** This is a culture in which groups, teams, or individual employees are rewarded for not asking difficult questions and for sticking to the script. They aren't asked for their opinions, and they don't feel comfortable speaking up. Leaders here are often surprised to learn what others feel and how it affects results. They don't ask their employees anything controversial, and their employees don't tell them anything. For such leaders, asking questions or encouraging critical thinking about a topic is seen as wasting time or decreasing efficiency.
- **Preserve harmony.** Many leaders believe that a quiet group is a productive group. They want to preserve harmony to give the impression that the group is well managed and a model for

organizational effectiveness. However, such groups are not likely to provide the innovation and ideas required to keep up in an increasingly competitive environment.

- **Tiptoe around a thin skin.** Some leaders are simply too thin-skinned to deal with the emotional fallout of conflict situations. They don't want to experience the disappointment, hurt feelings, and alienation that may come from encouraging constructive conflict. While understandable, this is not a good enough reason to avoid conflict.

EXAMPLE OF THE CONFLICT VOID

Jaysil is the client manager for one of the country's most recognized strategy consulting firms. Early in her career, she learned a costly lesson on how not to fall into the conflict void.

Jaysil was considered a star from the moment she joined the organization. She had a razor-sharp mind, worked harder than anyone else, and had a positive and optimistic approach to everything she did. As a result, she was given increasing levels of responsibility and eventually managed one of the firm's most important and demanding clients. Jaysil was both motivated by and afraid of the client's request to create a new strategy process that was untested by the organization. Even though it would give her an opportunity to be creative and exceed expectations, she knew that if the project failed, it would be challenging to recover from.

A host of complications marked the project from the beginning, including untested software requirements, miscommunication between the client and Jaysil's team, and poor chemistry between Jaysil and the client's project manager. But with tenacity and fortitude, Jaysil pressed on. She never mentioned the problems to her boss or that the project would end up considerably over budget. After much frustration and many wasted resources, the project ended up a colossal failure.

In a post mortem, Jaysil's boss asked her why she hadn't come to him (or the client, for that matter) to let them know that things were not going well. There had been many red flags and opportunities for Jaysil to alert all involved that their requests were unreasonable or that the project was way over budget. Jaysil, whose way of handling problems had always been to just work harder, had bitten off more than she could chew. She was uncomfortable having difficult conversations with her boss and her client, so instead of saying the hard things, Jaysil had avoided them. She kept quiet and continued to try to fix things.

Jaysil believed that the best project work moved efficiently but quietly, with everyone following the rules. She strove for a harmonious environment. She didn't want to see her boss's disappointment or argue with members on her project team. Further, members of her team didn't want to make their boss look bad to others, so instead of speaking up, they took the position that the client was being difficult. Jaysil had created a conflict void culture, and it didn't work.

When the project was concluded, the firm determined that Jaysil had spent three times more consulting hours and had doubled the cost quoted in the proposal. Needless to say, the client wasn't happy. Since she had avoided telling the client the bad news and handling the conflict that would surely have made resolving the issue possible, Jaysil's professional reputation took a significant hit.

The conflict void can interfere in many ways with an individual's or group's ability to perform at the highest level. Tolerating conflict is essential to achieving results. In other words, to be an effective leader, you need to toughen up and learn ways to manage a conflict to garner positive outcomes.

TIPS FOR MANAGING CONFLICT

As I mentioned in the beginning of this chapter, constructive conflict is necessary if leaders want to achieve exceptional results. In an ideal world, everyone would engage in robust debates when communicating and would ultimately deal with conflict in a healthy manner. But the world of work and the intense pressure that exists when leaders and their teams are asked to solve problems or come up with new and innovative solutions make the delicate balancing act of encouraging—and managing—conflict tricky at times, to say the least. In addition to conflict voids, conflict can also cause additional problems that will require courage to address and manage in a proactive manner. Here a few of the more common ones leaders should be aware of:

- **Handle a meeting bully.** Some people, despite organizational norms, tend to dominate conversations and advocate for their personal points of view. Their intensity shuts down other employees' opinions at meetings. The meeting bully's leader should coach him or her to temper the approach and advise the team on how to deal constructively with the bully. For example, a leader could say, "Joe, I hear and appreciate your point, but I want to make sure that everyone has a chance to share their point of view. Please hold your thoughts for a few moments until we have had a chance to hear from anyone else who may want to contribute their opinion." As a leader, you must model the right way to handle a meeting bully and demonstrate the courage to do so. You may also consider talking to this person in private to share your observations of his or her behavior. Be sure to let him or her know that his or her input is valuable; however he or she is in fact making it difficult for others to express their thoughts. Your meeting bully may very well be unaware of his or her behavior and will most likely welcome this feedback from you.

- **Control the pace.** A leader should always be mindful of whether a conflict is productive or not and be sensitive to how much conflict is right for any given situation. Healthy debate should always be encouraged, but there are certainly times when there is too much—or too little—conflict. For example, we have all been in meetings with a colleague who spends too much time expressing the same point of view about an issue in numerous ways. He or she is determined to get his or her point across but clearly is not effectively persuading others to his or her point of view. As a leader, you see that the rest of the group is becoming increasingly frustrated with this colleague who is now hindering the effectiveness of the team. Your job at this point is to step in and put a stop to this person's input. There are others times when a leader may in fact play "devil's advocate" and deliberately challenge his team to think of an issue in a different way. This is especially important if you feel that your group is on the verge of groupthink and may not be thinking of the issue with an appropriate level of analysis and depth. Your job is to arrive at the best results possible, and challenging your team to develop a wide variety of options is your duty. Techniques such as these will be essential in your efforts to problem solve at a level that fully utilizes your talents and of those you lead.
- **Ensure collective agreement.** After a conflict, if a complete collective understanding of what to do next is not reached and there

are still hard feelings, the conflict was mismanaged. Collective agreement is essential when there is conflict, just as it is in harmonious discussions. Leaders have to manage situations and keep a watchful eye for signs of alienation or disenchantment. It will be very important to manage collective agreement so that your team walks away from the situation feeling that they can support the direction decided upon even if the outcome was not what they desired. After conversations or discussions involving conflict, leaders should debrief participants and model and reward behaviors that help team members get past difficult discussions. Even if these are difficult conversations to have, leaders must engage in them with individuals who are having a hard time accepting outcomes generated after the conflict. Choosing not to do so will most likely result in conflict void. In particular, some individuals who have a hard time managing their emotions will likely share their negative feelings with others and may in fact undermine your efforts.

- **Don't allow lack of respect.** If a fundamental lack of respect is demonstrated in any discussion (name calling, yelling, or the like), the leader must take charge of the situation and insist on appropriate behavior. Not only is such behavior unprofessional, but it creates a culture where conflict void will fester. People who are open to engaging in healthy conflict will not feel safe enough to do so. It will be difficult to have mature conversations around difficult topics for fear that disrespectful people will fly off the handle and not be able to address the issues in an emotionally healthy manner. In a nutshell, real collaboration and the good outcomes that result from it will be difficult to generate. Finally, leaders who allow others to behave in a disrespectful manner will lose the trust of others, and their overall credibility and reputation as someone who can maintain control will be diminished.

CONSTRUCTIVE CONFLICT

Differing or opposing opinions can cause tension, uncomfortable feelings, or discord between individuals or teams. Good leaders understand that tension often leads to superior results, sharing of ideas, and individual professional growth. When it is managed well, conflict can be a useful tool to gain competitive advantage: it is constructive. When conflict is destructive or there is a conflict void, individuals and groups believe that harmony is the best way to get things done. Harmony is a good thing, but it should not be preserved at the expense of high-quality results.

Conflict tends to be constructive when:

1. Differing and opposing opinions are tolerated
2. Passionate feelings are allowed, but emotions are managed

3. The focus is on getting to a common end result

4. It is for the good of the person or group involved

BENEFITS OF CONSTRUCTIVE CONFLICT

The main benefit of constructive conflict is that it teaches people how to advocate for differing and opposing opinions without taking things personally. It also teaches leaders to differentiate between who a person is and the person's ideas. In addition, constructive conflict can help leaders find out what team members and groups really feel, not what they think the boss wants to hear. It encourages confidence by allowing people to stand up for their ideas without fear of rejection or reprisal. Finally, it helps to encourage a feedback-oriented culture, where anything can be said and discussed as long as it is done tactfully.

DEVELOPING A CULTURE THAT EMBRACES CONSTRUCTIVE CONFLICT

A culture that embraces constructive conflict is a safe place where questioning is tolerated from all levels of the organization. Junior employees can question senior ones without feeling the dividing line of organizational levels. Such a culture provides opportunities for discussing truths, even when they may be difficult to hear and even when it provokes people into sharing opinions that may feel uncomfortable.

For example, if an employee believes that your leadership style doesn't provide the discipline the group needs to be successful, he or she should feel comfortable tactfully communicating that to you, especially if the employee provides meaningful ideas on how to fix the problem.

Disagreements and displays of passion do not mean that your team is not effective. It is important to recognize that the tension of disagreement is a normal part of working together. As the leader, you must be able to control the temperature of those conversations without avoiding them. Include ample time for employees to voice their opinions, come to collaborative solutions, and leave the discussion in good spirits. Also, there should be a norm of respect for others' opinions, so that even if provocative or insulting words have been said, employees can give each other the benefit of the doubt. Employees should be comfortable with apologizing, and be encouraged to do so openly, when discussions get out of hand.

Constructive conflict requires a balance between respect for individuals and respect for their ideas. It is also necessary for all involved to support collective decisions, even if their own ideas are not chosen or their contributions to conversations did not persuade others. It should be an item in your code of conduct that members support the collective decisions that result from discussions, no matter how difficult doing so may be. If it is not, consider creating a group norm establishing that conflict around ideas is expected and that final outcomes are expected to be supported by all.

MASTERING CONSTRUCTIVE CONFLICT

If you are conflict-averse by nature, mastering constructive conflict may require you to learn new behaviors and skills. If you are motivated by the intensity of discussions that involve conflict, there are methods that can help you lead more effectively. It's important to master constructive conflict personally and to establish norms of constructive conflict for your organization.

Personally

If you feel that all conflict is bad, work to modify your values regarding it. Differentiate between constructive and destructive conflict, and learn techniques that can help you in conflict situations. For example:

- Prepare yourself for conversations that could give rise to conflict. Think through your arguments, anticipate responses, and have your own appropriate response ready if things go badly.
- If possible, determine others' perspectives beforehand so that you won't be caught off guard.

- Be ready to apologize and/or be influenced if the situation calls for it.

Culturally

Creating cultural norms that support constructive conflict requires you to

- articulate your point of view on constructive conflict and give others the permission to engage in it;
- openly reward others for questioning beliefs and organizational operations;
- model appropriate ways to confront and disagree with others; and
- correct those who don't adhere to appropriate conduct.

A PRESENTATION GONE BAD

A team of strategy analysts at a consumer products company was developing a presentation on customer retention for an internal client. After several months of tough going, the team generated its final conclusions, but it had often seemed to derail in the process: members complained that the project manager allowed too many opinions on the table and too much discussion.

At many meetings, analysts had argued, and there were hard feelings. But after each meeting, the team leader touched base with participants and let them know what they had done well—and poorly—in discussion. While he conveyed that the discussion had been good, he also noted that it was important to take the emotion out of it, that the discussions were not purely personal, and that all ideas needed to be heard. He reiterated that it was OK to be passionate about ideas and to defend them. He encouraged team members to become thick-skinned and not to take everything personally. He suggested that they should advocate for good ideas confidently, but also to let go of an idea if someone had a better one. Periodically, he insisted that the team engage in a social activity, like ordering dinner in as they worked. As the project moved forward, intense discussions continued and sometimes feelings would get hurt, but the leader's coaching had improved the team's ability to recover well.

When the team presented its findings to the customer, it garnered unprecedented approval. Team members reflected that, while the process of getting to the findings had been difficult and more time-consuming than some would have liked, the outcome would have been compromised without their sometimes contrary opinions. They came to believe that inherent in constructive conflict are many possibilities.

REALITY 8

Reputation is Everything
You Are Always On the Clock

Merriam-Webster defines reputation as an "overall quality or character as seen or judged by other people." In other words, it's your good name. Your reputation is the currency you will use to maintain your effectiveness and advancement as an executive. It is the most valuable characteristic you possess. It tells people how you are likely to behave and influences whether they trust you—or not. As such, you should guard your professional reputation as you would a priceless possession: once it is tarnished or lost, it can be impossible to recover.

The life of an executive is an open book in today's super-connected world. Employees, members of business and social communities, the media, and the like are extremely interested in what executives do both on and off the job. They constantly scrutinize, against incredibly high standards, how executives operate their lives, even in the personal sphere. The clubs executives join, their hobbies, and other extracurricular activities are of intense interest to many and discussed widely. The nature of the relationships executives have—and those they choose to have them with—are important to all with a vested interest in the company. This level of scrutiny is one of the highest prices executives have to pay for the privilege of leading, and it can often feel like an invasion of privacy.

THE HIGH PRICE OF LEADERSHIP

Executives pay another high price of public figures: the need to "walk the talk" at all times. The strength of an executive's reputation is determined by his or her ability to manage it to remain in favor with company stakeholders: executives must demonstrate their organizations' values both on and off the job. This seems like a very high price to pay for success, yet it is the reality of executive life.

Another high price leaders pay for the perks associated with C suite is the expectation that they should adhere to higher standards than others. "People don't like their leaders to have frailties. That's just the way it works," according to E. Allan Lind, professor of leadership at Duke University's Fuqua School of Business. [24] As we've seen, executives pay a high price for being in positions of power and influence: they are

---

[24] Sean Gregory, *Corporate Scandals: Why HP Had to Oust Mark Hurd,* http://www.time.com/time/business/article/0,8599,2009617,00.html?xid=rss-topstories (August 2010).

expected to live the values for which their companies stand. How much freedom to act and how much privacy an executive should have are frequently debated. Reasons that many believe strongly that executives must be held to the highest standards include:

- **Employees and stakeholders have a right to know about those who have power over them.** The decisions and judgment calls that executives make influence the health of the company and the livelihoods of its employees. Stakeholders want to know that they can trust their leaders to act in the best interests of all involved. When leaders do not act in accordance with the espoused values of an organization—both on and off the job—trust is breached and reputations can be tarnished, as well as the perception of the leader's effectiveness.

- **Personality characteristics are seen as generalizable.** If you have a lack of emotional control with your staff, it follows that you might also demonstrate the same weakness with the board of directors or when negotiating difficult situations. Negative personal characteristics like this in an executive can not only impact the perception of specific individuals but of the organization as a whole.

- **Executives were hired for skills and abilities that show they can represent the whole organization.** Therefore, they must remember that they are symbols that represent what the company stands for at all times.

- **Higher pay means greater accountability.** Being the face of an organization translates into bigger paychecks and larger perks for executives—but the pay is meant to compensate for the stress that comes with being in charge. However, the perception is that while average behavior is fine for an average employee with an average paycheck, bigger paychecks pay for a higher standard of behavior.

Even so, the lack of privacy and constant scrutiny that executives live under can be daunting, and like everyone else, they will make mistakes. Because their mistakes are often more visible and have greater consequences for so many, second chances may be hard to come by, depending on the degree of the hit to the executive's reputation. And while executives can't be expected to be superhuman, they are held to a higher standard and expected to be smart and savvy about the importance of their reputation. Following are several important pointers that leaders should be aware of as they navigate the complexities of reputation management in the C suite and beyond.

- **Nobody's perfect.** It's difficult for executives to be perfect, especially given the stress and pressure that characterize their lives. In fact, seeking stress alleviation can be the very reason for bad behavior off the job. Many forgive executives for going too far and feel that they should not be judged so harshly when they do.

- **Everyone deserves privacy.** Some people believe rules or norms should govern what is off limits to use for penalizing an executive on reputation. For example, should an executive who enjoys racing cars be seen as a thrill seeker and thus more likely to put the company at some kind of risk? Many believe it is possible to cleanly separate work and personal life and that everyone has a right to a private life and not to be judged for what they do in their free time—especially if they perform well at work and keep shareholders happy.

Overwhelmingly, however, people want their leaders to appear better than the rest of "regular" people. Unless they can see you this way, it is nearly impossible for them to trust and respect you as a leader, and certainly in more meaningful ways above and beyond the luxury car you drive. This is one of the prices you pay for being an executive with the ability to control the actions of others. You know you receive many advantages as an executive: respect, rewards, recognition, status, and adulation. However, that means you are also a symbol of what the organization is and wants to be. If you allow that symbol to become tarnished, there is a good chance the organization will become confused and embarrassed about who you are and what you represent. Your value system, and others' perceptions of what you stand for, will erode. This can have implications that can resonate throughout the entire organization. It is often said that with great power comes great responsibility: one of the greatest is making sure that your reputation — your currency — doesn't lose value and negatively impact your organization. Like all currencies, your reputation can grow in value or be devalued at any time by the activities you engage in, thus impacting your credibility as a leader both capable and worthy of leading an organization. Managing your reputation and making sure you maintain its value will be paramount for your long-term success.

PROTECTING YOUR REPUTATION

It takes a long time to create an unchallenged, rock-solid reputation. Your reputation says everything about who you are and what you stand for, how you want others to see you, what you want them to think about you, and what they can expect from you. *Reputation is predictive.* It makes people feel safe, because they can predict how you are likely to behave, even when no one is looking.

Your job as an executive is to actively and constantly protect your reputation and to defend it when necessary. If tarnished, it is difficult — if not impossible — to repair. Consider the following to protect your reputation.

- **Select an organization that shares your personal values.** If being inclusive and open to new ideas is a personal value of yours, make sure that you join an organization that values the same ideals. Write a personal statement that specifically answers the question: "What do I want others to say when they talk about me?" Frequently quiz others, both in and outside of your organization, to see how well you measure up to what you want others to think about you.

- **Learn the spoken and unspoken values and norms in your company.** Watch what your company's executives do during and after working hours. Listen to how they communicate, both casually and formally. If your executives don't use foul language, then you shouldn't either. If making charitable contributions is a part of your executive culture, then consider those that would be most appropriate for you.

- **Make a strong commitment to your organization and its success.** Commitment to your organization's success helps to ensure that you proactively manage your reputation well. It means that you care about the impact your actions can have on your company, its mission, its customers, and its employees. If you can't commit to your organization, you may not pay as much attention to your reputation as you should. It is easier to commit if you work for a company with a leadership team you can respect, a company mission you believe in, and people you enjoy working with.

WAYS THAT EXECUTIVES RUIN THEIR REPUTATIONS

Managing your reputation is clearly an important part of managing your professional career, yet many leaders engage in activities that they know can undermine their reputations and impact those to whom they are closest. Take former CIA director David Petraeus for example. Shortly after Barack Obama was reelected president of the United States in 2012, Petraeus wrote to his employees that he had "showed extremely poor judgment by engaging in an extramarital affair." Although the four-star general was praised by the president and other influential political leaders for his outstanding contribution to the country, debate ensued in the press as to whether his personal missteps should reflect negatively on the value he brought to his job. Mr. Petraeus's lack of judgment off the job ruined his reputation; his once-promising career in public service is likely to be over.

In the same year, fast-food restaurant company Chick-Fil-A went under fire when its COO, Dan Cathy, made statements that offended gays and lesbians. NBC News affiliate WPTV.com reported Mr. Cathy as saying, "We are very much supportive of the family—the biblical definition of the family unit. We are a family-owned business, a family-led business, and we are married to our wives first." Clearly, Cathy was not in favor of same-sex marriage; politicians in Chicago and New York encouraged a boycott of Chick-Fil-A. Some gay and lesbian employees said they were surprised by the COO's comments; meanwhile, some customers and a toy manufacturer broke with the company. Some students whose schools had Chick-Fil-A shops wanted them to leave. What the COO said mattered. While he did not lose his job, the restaurant had to handle distracting (and likely costly) public relations and branding issues.

Of course, executives may believe that what they do on their personal time is their business, and to a large degree this is true. However, consider what happened to an executive who belonged to a country club that did not admit women, African Americans, or Jews. Although no one really believed that the executive himself was a racist or a bigot, they didn't understand why he belonged to this club. As word spread about his membership, the support within the organization that he'd always relied on began to wane, and he found that he was not able to advance. He eventually resigned from the club, but the damage had been done. His colleagues and superiors had questioned his judgment and had seen him in a different, unflattering light.

These stories illustrate an important lesson in reputation management: the intent of your actions is less important than others' perception of them. Other types of behaviors you should avoid so that you can keep the trust and respect of your professional and personal peers include:

- **Engaging in inappropriate relationships.** Many view inappropriate relationships as signs of poor judgment and an inability to honor commitment. If you are single and engage in a relationship with someone in your company, you should always disclose that to leadership. Some companies frown upon fraternization between employees, but others just want to avoid putting you in a position where you are responsible for rewarding and recognizing someone with whom you are involved.

- **Airing your political and religious views.** Everyone is entitled to their religious and political views, but when you are an executive, it is probably best if you keep them to yourself. Your views on these matters can alienate you from others, and if they are inconsistent with corporate views, they can be embarrassing for you and the company.

- **Joining associations inconsistent with your organization's values.** People usually join clubs that are consistent with the lifestyles they live, but if any of your associations excludes others based on gender, race, ethnic background, and the like, you run the risk of being viewed negatively. No one wants to support a leader who belongs to a club that excludes them for reasons that the company wouldn't.

- **Being indiscreet in casual conversations.** Be careful to whom you talk about company business and colleagues. At a beauty salon, an executive of a sportswear retailing company once heard a woman give excruciatingly negative details about a colleague — and their company's strategy — for an hour. The woman did not know that she was sitting next to an executive from her own company. Needless to say, the woman's reputation was tarnished due to her lack of discretion and respect for the company. Sharing impromptu comments with the media is another way to converse without proper forethought and insight, as many a former employee can attest.

• **Displaying unbecoming behavior.** Behavior inappropriate to a mature person who is a role model for others in a company may ruin an executive's reputation. This includes aggressive and foul language in public places and in private gatherings, aggressive driving, excessive alcohol consumption (even on your own time), allowing provocative photographs to be taken of you, sloppy attire, and a poor choice of places to spend your time (e.g., bars and strip clubs). Behaviors such as these provide ripe opportunities for others to scrutinize your actions—and to question your values.

• **Using social media unwisely.** How an executive uses social media matters. In fact, it is in most executives' best interest to use social media outlets like Facebook, LinkedIn, Twitter, Instagram, and the like sparingly. Have professionals help you to use social media outlets to benefit you—to enhance your reputation as an expert, promote your organization, or share your commitment to philanthropic causes. While it may be tempting to try, you should never assume you can live separate personal and professional social media lives. At this level of the game, everything you say and do is intertwined. The personal impacts the professional, and vice versa.

- **Using voice mail, e-mails, and text messages unwisely.** Be mindful of not only the language you use in voice mail, e-mails, and text messages but also what you choose to communicate with them. Never send any of these when you feel emotional about a topic. Use these channels to communicate facts and information. Err on the side of person-to-person exchanges for sharing important information. A provocative e-mail, text message, or voice mail that you initiate can find its way throughout your organization—or even wind up in the hands of someone external to your organization or in the media—in record time.

REBUILDING YOUR REPUTATION

If you have the misfortune of tarnishing your reputation, there are steps you can take to restore it. First, you must recognize that your reputation is at risk or has been tarnished. Most successful executives continuously seek feedback on the perception of their behavior and their performance. Here are a few options to consider if you have to rebuild your reputation:

- **Prepare a strategy for damage control.** Think about the circumstances that led to the ruin of your reputation. Whom do you need to convince that your actions were a mistake and that you deserve a second chance to repair the situation and your reputation? More than anything, you need patience to see it all through and manage your own expectations about how much time is needed for recovery. The truth is, it takes as long as it takes. But you can help it along: be sincere and consistent in your behavior, and add new behaviors to your repertoire to dilute the old and unacceptable behaviors that got you into trouble in the first place. Finally, practice self-insight and ask yourself if you are likely to repeat the behaviors that damaged your reputation. If so, then you should be prepared to accept the consequences and your reputation's inevitable permanent ruin.

• **Apologize.** Apologies are a delicate matter. Sometimes they are necessary, such as when you bully an employee in a meeting. But at other times, apologies can make you look even more unattractive as a leader and actually worsen your reputation by casting a negative light on your judgment. Consider the following story. A vice president of sales in a consulting firm made a reputational mistake that caused others in the company to doubt his emotional control. His son was a great soccer player at the local high school. One day, the son missed a goal at the playoffs, and the VP aggressively yelled at him and shoved him to the ground. The VP had been well known in the community and had even been considering running for mayor. After this incident, however, his former supporters no longer saw him as a trustworthy authority figure, both personally and professionally. In an effort to maintain his reputation, he quickly made a public apology for his behavior, but truthfully, he probably should simply have resigned. Doing so would have sent the message that he understood that he acted incorrectly, was not suitable to run for mayor or maintain his present position, and took full responsibility for his actions. You may need to make a similar call either way. As an executive, being able to apologize and show real remorse for a wrongdoing is an essential and important first step toward rebuilding your tarnished reputation.

WHEN RECOVERING YOUR REPUTATION ISN'T POSSIBLE

Even under the best of circumstances, recovering from a mistake that damages your reputation is very difficult. While business books are full of stories about executives who made mistakes and recovered and rebuilt their reputation over time, sometimes recovery from a reputational faux pas is not possible.

When an organization withdraws its support from you in a way that makes you feel you are no longer integral to it, or when getting your job done appears difficult, chances are pretty good that you are not likely to recover. When you have embarrassed yourself and your organization to the point where others are uncomfortable being around you, recovery is also very unlikely. It's probably best then to cut your losses, learn from your mistakes, and use what you've learned to be a better leader in another organization.

Finally, if you receive poor feedback from your employees and your reputation takes a hit because of it, your boss may give you a chance to recover while holding his or his opinion of you in reserve. If you are truly capable and committed to doing the job well and addressing the issues uncovered in the feedback you got, you may be able to rebuild your reputation and regain the open support of your boss.

FINAL THOUGHTS

Managing your reputation should be a proactive part of your long-term career planning and development. It requires foresight and the ability to see the big picture and how your behaviors, small or large, can potentially impact every sphere of your personal and professional life. With that in mind:

- **Do not assume that your personal and professional lives are separate and distinct.** What you do on and off the job will have an impact on your reputation and future opportunities available to you in your company. The type of organization you work for can also impact how well you can recover from a reputational mistake. In a company with conservative corporate values, it may be nearly impossible to restore your reputation. In more flexible corporate environments, you may be given the opportunity to restore your reputation, though it will still take time. Either way, if you keenly observe what your leaders and colleagues do versus what they say, you may be able to predict whether you can successfully restore your reputation.

- **Understand that rebuilding a tarnished reputation takes a great deal of time and patience.** When your reputation has been tarnished and is at stake, acting angry or belligerent about being misjudged or misunderstood only makes things worse and impacts your ability to recover. If you have behaved in a way that's out of character—whether on or off the job—be patient and take the high road. Strive to prove to others that you can be trusted again. Your actions may have made it difficult for others to predict your behavior, and this uncertainty makes your relationship with them a bit challenging until you fully recover. Try to understand that people's faith in you has been rocked. While it may be difficult to rebuild your reputation, it can be done—but it takes time and patience. You must believe in others' ability to draw the right conclusions about you through observing your consistent effort over time.

- **Understand that you can't always rebuild or restore a reputation.** Perhaps your company protects itself with a culture that holds on to employee missteps for a long time. Maybe people in the organization just won't allow you to recover and move forward. It might be best to leave your company, but you could remain and hope for the best. As with all judgment calls, there is a certain amount of risk, but it is generally not a good idea to remain in a company where you are better known for a mistake that you have actively tried to rectify than for your current performance and contributions.

Finally, remember that managing your reputation should receive the same care you give to managing your retirement portfolio. Check in on it regularly, and ask others for feedback often. More importantly, don't take it for granted.

REALITY 9

The Company Can't Love You Back
So Get a Life

As a leader, it is incredibly easy to become seduced by your importance and the control you have over your activities and those of others—so much so, that many leaders forget to make a life for themselves. Yet, it has been proven time and time again that if you make your job your life, you run the risk of feeling terribly disappointed, abandoned, and even depressed, because as much as you may love your job, the company can't love you back. People can love you back, but companies cannot.

It is so important for leaders to maintain interests and relationships that are not solely based on their jobs. Leaders who have lives outside of their jobs are more likely to demonstrate mature and appropriate behaviors in the workplace. They don't put undue pressure on the organization to meet personal needs that should be met elsewhere. When leaders look to their jobs and colleagues for the satisfaction and emotional support that they should receive from family and friends, they tend to magnify the disappointments they experience and the expectations they have of other people. They seek promotions or expect accolades to make them feel excited about life. Some feel "stuck" in life and that their job is either the cause or the solution.

A LIFE OF DENIAL

Charlie is a Columbia Business School graduate who landed a coveted position in the marketing department of an international pharmaceutical company. Over ten years, he advanced to positions of increasing responsibility and was classified as being high potential. He was on the track to become an officer of the company. Charlie attributed most of his success to putting his job first. While he married and had two kids along the way, he prided himself on the fact that his performance and accessibility never decreased with changes in his personal life.

As Charlie's responsibilities increased, he was asked to mentor junior high-potential employees, to serve on special committees, and to represent the company at business conferences. A few of the jobs Charlie was promoted into were stressful and required considerable travel. He gained some weight and had trouble sleeping, but he understood them as a price he had to pay to get to the top. His wife began to complain that he was an absentee father and husband, but he thought that the job was all worth it: he provided for his family and made a major contribution to his organization. He made a few close friends at work but fell out of touch with other friends.

Charlie didn't feel as if he was missing anything, though; he felt very connected to his job and his company. In fact, he felt fortunate and never really questioned the direction of his life. Charlie felt successful—more than others with whom he had gone to college. He trusted the senior leadership team and felt secure in putting all he had into his work. The company had never let him down, and he would not let it down.

At one meeting, after a decade of loyal service, Charlie's boss told him that his division was being relocated to London and that his counterpart there would be taking over his responsibilities. Charlie was made redundant and was out of a job. At first, he was in denial. He didn't tell his wife immediately, because he was certain that he could turn the situation around. Charlie's boss was appropriately distressed by what had happened; by all accounts, Charlie was a highly valued, dedicated, and effective employee. He told Charlie not to feel at fault and that there was nothing he could have done—or could do now. It had been a strategic decision for the good of the business. Charlie knew that the organization had hired a strategy firm months earlier to help position the business for the future, but he had never considered that he could be a casualty of its new strategic direction.

Charlie was stunned when he found he couldn't repair his situation; he felt completely betrayed. In his mind, he had given his company his all, and just like that, it was over. He didn't have time to transition psychologically or emotionally from working for the company to not working at all. Charlie felt estranged from his workplace friends of the past ten years and was uncomfortable asking them for comfort or support. He hadn't really networked outside of the organization and was not current on external opportunities. He was not in the best shape to handle an interview process, anyway. He felt stuck, depressed, and completely unsuccessful, even though he had exceptional skills and capabilities.

Leaders like Charlie are often seduced by the rewards that come from high-level work and collaboration with organization colleagues: smart people have to listen to what you say and do what you ask; your job title gives you permission to make things happen — and considerable control over your life and the work lives of others. It can be a heady experience. But Charlie lost his perspective, partly because he abdicated his life to the company and forgot that the company might not always be there for him. Just because you are successful does not guarantee that you'll get the reward you expect for it.

Remember that organizations actively create an illusion that you are part of a family. Some companies suggest that they are so much better than all of their peers and that it would be a waste of your time to consider another organization...ever. The commitment that organizations make to leaders in an attempt to build morale and cohesion can be misinterpreted. It needs to be taken in the spirit in which it is given. Never forget that most organizations exist to meet the needs of their stakeholders. While companies do seek to satisfy employees' expectations to some degree, your needs will not likely supersede the needs of an organization. For strategic or big-picture reasons, it may be in the organization's best interest to fire you, retire you, demote you, or reduce your salary. At the core of the employee-company relationship is an exchange of services for pay. When a company no longer needs your services, it is required to stop paying you for them.

As a result of the blind faith that many leaders place in the organization and the organization's attempts to keep them motivated and committed, many leaders neglect their families, personal development, and health. These executives have no idea what their marketability is within the work world and often wouldn't know where to start to look for a new job. They leave little time for networking outside of the company or building relationships with influential others outside of their organization. All of these mistakes result in leaders' feelings of betrayal when there is a sudden negative shift in their work worlds.

RECOGNIZING WHEN YOUR JOB IS YOUR LIFE

Often, a leader doesn't recognize when the job is his or her life. Such leaders get accustomed to working all the time and think that giving all their time to the job is a necessary sacrifice to be in a leadership position. It's not.

Signs that can tell you when your job has become your life include:

- The only relationships you've developed over the past ten years are with co-workers
- All of your friends work at your company
- Your family is constantly complaining about your lack of availability
- You have no hobbies or interests outside of work
- You rarely take your vacation time
- You are available around the clock to answer e-mails and texts regarding work
- Your conversations after work hours are all about work
- When you think about a future without the company, you feel helpless and scared
- You have no idea what you are worth in the marketplace or where else you might work

The distinction between being committed and loyal to your company and making your company your life is important. One suggests that you, as a leader, have some control over the situation; the other suggests that you've given control of your life to your company.

LEADING AS AN ENRICHING PART OF A FULFILLING LIFE

As a leader, you should have certain expectations of your organization—that it will employ you forever is not one of them! But you should expect your organization to provide you with the following:

- **Professional Development.** You should expect to be given the time, support, and resources you require to keep yourself current as a leader. You don't want to become obsolete, and the company shouldn't want that either. Annual leadership development experiences are not uncommon. If your company can't provide them for you, then seek them in your community. You can also read and study about leaders, join nonprofit community boards, and seek opportunities to speak in community settings.
- **Honesty.** You should know where you stand. If you're in trouble as a leader, you should not be the last to know. If the

organization is in trouble, then you should be given enough information to make informed decisions about your life.

- **Time Off.** You should not be made to feel ineffective if you take your vacation. You should be an example to those who report to you; encourage them to take vacations as well. It is important for all of you to be able to rest and rejuvenate.

- **Community Contributions.** It is important for leaders to contribute to their communities, and companies should support that; contribution is good for the company and the individual. It puts you in touch with other community leaders, and it gives you an opportunity to develop as a leader and a chance to give back.

GET A LIFE

You should make it part of your personal philosophy to have a full and complete life. Family, relationships, community involvement, and hobbies are all important aspects of a fulfilling life. Do these for yourself:

- **Rejuvenate.** This bears repeating: take your vacations. Manage your leadership responsibilities so that you can take vacations or time off to recharge and rejuvenate. This helps ensure that you are healthy, both physically and mentally.

- **Participate actively in your family life.** Strong family lives provide a great deal of emotional support and a broader sense of value for many. When crises hit, you should turn to family and close friends for support, not the organization.

- **Find a hobby that brings you joy and pleasure.** Hobbies make you a more interesting person and provide you with an outlet for stress. If you have a difficult time deciding on a hobby, think back to activities you enjoyed when you were younger. This might be a good time to take them up again.

- **Know what you're worth.** It is not disloyal to know your marketability. You should always know where key opportunities exist in your field and network with those in positions of authority and responsibility.

Always remember that no matter how important your position, you are dispensable. Use this information to motivate yourself to be sensible about your relationship with your organization. You don't have to expect your organization to disappoint you. You just want to be prepared if it does.

REALITY 10

When Your Time is Up
Knowing When to Leave the Party

Every executive in a job will eventually leave it. It doesn't matter how great the job is, whether the company is the perfect fit for you, or how well liked and well regarded you are. Eventually, one day, you will have to leave. In the best-case scenario, you can predict when your time has come and will have considerable control over how and when you depart. You can increase the possibility if you give a great deal of thought and planning to create a vision of how you want to leave. A vision that guides how you want to depart from your current role actually sets you up for a flawless transition out of the job, prepares you for the next opportunity, and can actually be a gratifying experience.

The notion of planning for your exit may seem counterintuitive, especially if you are enjoying success in your current role, are well regarded at work, or simply like what you do (and the people around you). Whether you are an executive who grew up in your company or you were hired from outside, many believe that if you focus on leaving, you can't really be focused on the job at hand. That's like saying that if you prepare for death by engaging in estate planning, you must not be very interested in living. Neither is true. Thinking about how you want to leave your role from the beginning actually provides you with the comfort of more control over your career and work experience.

When you have thought through and identified the conditions that signal you can no longer be effective in the job, you can quickly recognize them when they emerge in your work environment and act appropriately. This minimizes the possible feelings of betrayal, anger, and loss most individuals experience when things don't go as planned, simply because you are not surprised. You will be able to see the issue as more of a process than an event and to act rather than just react.

A CHANGE IN THE LANDSCAPE

Consider the story of Oscar Stone. Oscar was the vice president of sales for a household-name pharmaceutical company. He felt surprised and betrayed by his CEO when he was replaced by a well-regarded regional manager whom Oscar had trained.

Oscar didn't see it coming. He had always enjoyed a personal friendship with his boss and felt that he would get a heads-up if he was in trouble. Even though Oscar knew that the sales numbers were not tracking the way they should, he also knew that everyone felt he had a solid team, years of experience, and an unwavering twenty-year commitment to the company. And anyway, there were broader business issues impacting Oscar's ability to get results. The company's competitive landscape had recently changed when a generic version of the company's blockbuster drug was introduced to the marketplace, and a long-awaited drug in the company's pipeline was slow to gain approval from the FDA. Oscar felt that the company understood those challenges and had already committed himself to overcome them, as always.

But, if Oscar was honest, he would admit that about a year before these challenges surfaced, he'd begun to feel anxiety and uncertainty about his job. His numbers were down, yes, but that was only part of it. Company morale had slipped, and he was asked what he planned to do to improve morale on his team. As Oscar faced his challenges, the CEO had retained a strategy consulting group to realign the organization's structure, initiated 360-degree feedbacks on all senior leaders, spent more time in Germany with the parent company's leadership team—and worked more closely with Oscar's direct reports.

Oscar was not invited to participate in the CEO's strategy consultant meetings, though he felt he should have been. The exclusion coincided with an almost imperceptible change in how senior people in the organization treated him. Impromptu elevator conversations were shorter, and there was less laughter. In addition, he felt that others were privy to information that he didn't have about topics he used to be kept in the loop about. Oscar once asked his boss if everything was all right and if he should be worried about losing his job. His boss assured him that even though these were trying times, he appreciated Oscar's contributions. After that conversation, Oscar decided that the best thing he could do was to focus on getting results and ignore the nagging feeling that something was terribly wrong.

Two months later, Oscar was fired, with little fanfare—and, as Oscar would put it, with very little acknowledgment that he had sacrificed much of his life for the company. At first, he was stunned—and then paralyzed by the feeling of being used. Most important, he was plagued by the question, "If I'm such a good executive, how did I get myself into this situation?"

Oscar took a new position that he immediately realized was a mistake and left after only a year. His self-esteem began to take a dive, and he was no longer satisfied with his life. Oscar, an upbeat and optimistic individual by nature, began to obsess about the reasons he was let go and others weren't. His firing was all he talked about. It began to negatively impact his career. Even people who cared about him avoided him; they wanted him to move on. Oscar eventually got another good job, but there was a bitterness about him that made it difficult for him to perform to his usual satisfying level. His trust in the relationship between a corporation and its leaders had been eroded, and he lost the amazing motivation and positive attitude that had always been the backbone of his success.

As with Oscar, many executives put the fate of their futures solely in the hands of a company, its leadership, and its policies and procedures. They trust the organization to let them know when it is time to leave and how they should do it. They often ignore their gut instincts and signs that indicate there is a problem. The best executives know the difference between insignificant signs that can be ignored and those that can't. They also know when—because they watch for an accumulation of certain, specific factors—no matter what they are being told, it is time to go.

In other words, it's always important to know when it's time to leave a party. Before you go to a party, you probably have a clear idea of the type of experience you want to have. You might want to meet new people, network with professional acquaintances, or hang out with good friends. In your vision of the perfect party experience, you don't want to be the last to leave: the buffet has been picked over, the floor is sticky from spilled drinks, there are no more clean glasses, the music has ended, and all the interesting guests have left. You want to leave the party when things are going well and you still feel good about your experience. So, going in, you need to have an idea when to call it a night and head home!

Similarly, you have to know when it's time to leave a job. We'll tell you how to leave your job on your terms with your head held high, but also what to do when you've stayed too long and are asked to leave.

YOUR DEPARTURE CREED AND PRINCIPLES

Before you enter a leadership position, define for yourself the rules, beliefs, and conditions that indicate it is time to leave. These principles make up your "departure creed" and help you notice when things are not going according to plan and that perhaps your departure is imminent, even though some in the organization want you to stay. Examples of what to include in your departure creed might be:

1. I will leave when I no longer feel valuable, regardless of what I am told.
2. I will leave when my work is not challenging and when there are no real opportunities for advancement or professional or personal growth.
3. I will leave when I no longer trust my organization's leadership.
4. I will leave when the organization breaks any of my deal-breaker values.
5. I will leave when I am being marginalized.
6. I will leave when I feel that I have to hide most of who I am.
7. I will leave when I feel like a fake.
8. I will leave when I cannot get accurate feedback from others.

9. I will leave when getting my job done is increasingly difficult.

10. I will leave when my commute is too long.

11. I will leave when I've done the most that I can in my role. I won't be lazy, just sit in a job, and become a blocker.

12. I will leave when the quality of my work life is bad.

13. I will leave when I really want to do something else.

14. I will leave when I've done all I could to make a difference.

15. I will leave when I cannot make a difference.

16. I will leave when I begin to feel like an outsider.

17. I will leave if the value proposition of the company is in bad shape and I don't believe that it can be remedied.

18. I will leave if I can honestly say that I hate my job.

19. I will leave if being good at my job means that I don't have a life.

20. I will leave if I'm staying only because I'm afraid to go.

Review your departure principles at least annually. If you find that three or more of the negative conditions they outline apply, then it may well be time for you to leave the party. Your own departure principles may include items from the above list, but you may have others. The important thing is to document them, revisit them, and let them guide your decision to depart or anticipate departure.

SHANIA'S DEPARTURE

Shania had been heavily recruited to be the head of human resources at a financial services institution and got an amazing compensation package. She had extraordinary interpersonal skills; she liked people and focused her energy on bringing out the best in others. It was no surprise to anyone that she was shortly able to garner support from all parts of the company.

Even though things were going well, after a few months in her new role, Shania realized that her assignments were well below her capabilities. She liked her co-workers, but the work itself was just not challenging. She told herself that she was making a difference—and she certainly was. Her pay motivated her to keep looking for the best in her job.

Over time, Shania interacted more with the CEO and her peers. She was surprised by how informally business was conducted at the senior level. She told herself that as long as she wasn't asked to do anything that compromised her integrity, everything would be OK. Even so, she had a nagging feeling that the leadership team had some problematic ethical issues.

Shania had a lot to gain by staying in her job. She was highly compensated for doing what she knew. It would be years before the organization presented her with a challenge that she hadn't seen. Deep inside, though, she knew that she couldn't stay, even if the company wanted her to.

Eventually, as she had predicted might happen, the CEO made a request of Shania that she could not support. She knew it would harm certain people and would negatively impact employee morale. The request was not for anything illegal; it simply went against her personal values, so she refused. While the CEO said that he understood, Shania knew there would be consequences. She developed a mindset based on her values and didn't take anything personally.

Shania knew that she would have to leave behind the company, the big salary, and the perks. Her main concern was how to do it so that she came out of it OK. First, she went about tightening up the loose ends in her department. Then, she contacted a headhunter to see what opportunities were percolating in the region. Shania reviewed her personal budget and cut back on her spending, just in case she needed to conserve money soon. She alerted her family that things were not going as well as expected on her job and that she was thinking about next steps. This was important, since Shania's salary was essential to her household.

Shania also had a tough conversation with herself about what was really happening. In essence, she began to think through her departure principles. The problem represented a significant gap between what she needed from the company and what it could provide. For Shania, the gap was not likely to close. She faced a lack of challenging work, differences with the company's values at the top, and the fact that she'd never felt comfortable in her role.

As Shania had predicted, the CEO scheduled a meeting with her four months later, where he and the company's lawyer fired her. The reasons were efficiently outlined in a letter. But since Shania had expected that she would soon be asked to leave, she was prepared. She calmly told the firing squad that she would review their letter and their proposed severance package with her own lawyer and would get back to them shortly. With good form, she wished them well as individuals and prosperity for the company.

Shania's preparedness allowed her to avoid the shock, drama, and emotional meltdown that often accompany such situations and to focus her energies on the departure deal. Shania's departure principles had prepared her well for exiting the organization, dignified and composed.

SIGNALS THAT IT'S TIME TO DEPART

There are always signs that it is time to leave a job. Sadly, though, many leaders say they "never saw it coming," and they struggle with feelings of anger and betrayal long after they leave. Of course, such a statement suggests that the leader wasn't a good one at all. A leader *should* see it coming, but most don't, because their egos or fears are in the way. Remember that an organization's cultural norms don't lie. If you learn the norms at your firm, you can read the signs. If you don't know them or you consistently operate outside of them, there is a high probability that you will be asked to leave—and that it will be an unpleasant surprise. Signs that indicate it may just be time for you to leave include:

A VOTE OF NO CONFIDENCE (THE ORGANIZATION'S REASONS).

If some decision you make causes a functional or enterprise-wide failure and you cannot recover from it, plan for your departure. You may have added considerable value since the poor decision, or even corrected it, but if your failure has become part of your professional identity and you are reminded of it in conversations and performance reviews—discreetly or not—you cannot afford to ignore the signs. Some organizations just won't allow mistakes to be forgotten. In succession planning discussions, you will be at a disadvantage, and it will be nearly impossible for you to reach your full potential.

OVERALL DISSATISFACTION (YOUR REASONS).

If you consistently feel a general sense of dissatisfaction in your leadership role, consider leaving it. Leadership job dissatisfaction is evident, no matter how you try to mask it. You should ask yourself why you stay if you're so unhappy. You look weak as a professional: you lack the courage and wherewithal to sort out your own situation. You do yourself and the organization a favor by leaving.

Dissatisfied leaders who can't seem to find the right mix of what makes them feel good about their work act out in a variety of ways. Not only does their performance deteriorate, but they also make unreasonable requests of the organization, poison the minds of others in it, and overstep organizational boundaries. Although these leaders will be asked to leave, it is sometimes only after they've done irreparable damage to their reputations, bastardizing their brands.

If you are under the impression that your superiors don't trust you or believe that you can't handle the job, consider leaving. Your senior leaders have given you a vote of no confidence, and trust is hard to regain, even under the best of circumstances. Signs of a no-confidence vote include being micromanaged, being incrementally stripped of roles or responsibilities, or getting ambiguous answers in conversations about your future with higher-ups.

LACK OF FIT WITH THE CULTURE (OUTSIDE REASONS).

The "perfect fit" you and your company first felt for each other can change and not feel so perfect anymore. This can occur when a significant change impacts the culture, such as a merger or acquisition. The organization may want you to act in a way that compromises your personal values, or it makes a fundamental shift in the way it approaches its business and customers. Changes of this nature often signal that it may be time to look elsewhere for a new opportunity.

There are several reasons the perfect fit can erode. Let's say that though your company gained its long-term, loyal customers by educating them on products and benefits, shrinking market share has now made selling more important than educating customers, and your deep expertise is no longer valued. Or, your organization is acquired in the hope of becoming stronger, and your job is duplicated. But because of your great expertise, the company wants you to stay — only in a lesser job with less responsibility. The acquiring company knows you are a valuable asset but has no need for you in your current role, so it holds onto you until it finds a place for your talents or until it can't afford to keep you. Companies, like people, often keep things they don't need, "just in case." Yet you, as a leader, should read the signs: it's time to leave for an opportunity where you and your contributions add clear value. You are not a showpiece that no longer makes a real impact.

These signs may not seem awful enough to make you leave, but if you are not very clearly satisfied in your job, it is in your best interest to begin your departure strategy. Don't become the dusty executive on the shelf. You deserve better than that.

THE COURAGE TO PLAN: *WHAT ARE YOU AFRAID OF?*

It's natural to be nervous about building a departure strategy, let alone executing on it. It draws on your higher-order leadership capabilities: you must be insightful enough to see the big picture of your career, strategic enough to develop a plan, and courageous enough to put it into action for the good of the organization and yourself. Thinking about how you will leave your job is not a bad thing; it is essential.

- **Be honest with yourself.** Your own insights about what you need from your career and the organization's transparency regarding your value will give you most of the information you need to determine if you should initiate a departure strategy. Figure out what you really want, and learn to read the cues your organization gives.

- **Be confident that you can be effective in other jobs and environments.** You always have options. As soon as you think you are not marketable, you can bet that your company doesn't see you as a rock star either. People who consider their options and what they can do next—even as a stopgap measure—are in a better position to initiate departure plans when needed.

- **Don't overstay your welcome.** Can you imagine what it would be like if everyone in your college class graduated and left to pursue careers, yet two years later, you are still hanging around on campus? If you look around and find that your peers have all been promoted to bigger and broader responsibilities while you feel stuck, it is time to go. Stay with your class—or excel beyond it. But don't get left behind.

- **Believe in yourself.** If you are to have a rewarding leadership experience, you have to believe that you deserve one. If you have to leave a position, don't whine about it. Keep your head up and make it happen. Often, the decision to leave turns into something very positive.

RISKS AND OBSTACLES

Of course, leaving a job is risky—especially if you don't have a new one lined up already. You might wonder if you're leaving too soon or have made the wrong decision. If you've done your homework and have a good plan in place, a wrong decision is highly unlikely. And besides, if you are a strong executive, you will land on your feet. Sometimes you can't see what's waiting for you until you get certain things out of the way. If you feel that leaving means responsibilities are left unhandled, you have not planned well and should delay departure until everything is in good hands. (Hopefully, your company isn't insistent on your departure and it's at least mostly your choice.)

This chapter is not about ruining your life; it's about taking control of it. Use your common sense. I've seen many executives leave on what appears to be a spur-of-the-moment decision, yet land on their feet successfully. Usually, it's because they were aware of their situation and had a planned exit strategy that allowed them the freedom to choose when they departed, but sometimes, they just seized the moment. The whole point of departure principles is that you are always aware of where you stand, because sometimes the best time to leave the party comes suddenly.

The idea that you might not be able to get a new leadership position of the same size and scope can be very daunting. This fear keeps many people stuck in jobs that just don't work. Some executives, though, take "smaller" and perhaps different jobs than the ones they left because the new organization is a better fit. While the new job may not carry the same status, these leaders may enjoy the challenge of working in a new industry, with different types of leaders, or within a more challenging economy. Think about the quality of the leadership position and not just its status. The money usually follows, even if it takes longer to reach earlier compensation and benefit levels.

FINAL THOUGHTS

When planning your departure, consider what is best for you *and* for the organization. As a responsible leader, it is appropriate for you to maintain a genuine interest in and responsibility for both.

Once you know that you have to depart, you should ready the organization for your departure, too. That does not mean you should tip your hand, but you should tie up loose ends and prepare to hand the reins of your job to someone else. Make the transition as easy as you can by creating plans and documentation that allow a new person to pick up from where you left off. Think too about what you would like people to say about you once you leave, and work to make this perception a reality. For example, if you want others to say that you were a strong, high-integrity leader with concern for employees and the organization, then make sure that you pursue your goals and objectives as close to completion as possible.

Strive to leave with the same positive attitude you had when you started. It's a mistake to get carried away with emotion when you realize you need to leave or are asked to leave. Not only do emotional departures demand energy and unsettle everyone around you, but they also undermine your leadership brand. Leave blame and anger by the wayside. Neither serves much of a purpose.

View leaving as a natural phase in the cycle of your work career. If you embrace it, you will more clearly see the benefits and opportunities that await you in your new future.

Final Words of Wisdom

We hope you've enjoyed the ideas and observations in this book. More important, we hope that at least one concept, rule, or example caused you to have an "aha" moment. Our goal was not to be the final authority on leadership; the true essence of leadership cannot be explained, explored, or shared in any one book. Rather, our goal was to share a "sneak peek" into the lessons and challenges of senior leadership and to help prepare the next generation of senior leaders in some small way.

The reality of today's business environment demands that leaders are prepared to not only deal with growing the bottom line but also leverage an organization's most valuable asset: its human capital. Faced with a complex global economy, continuous technological innovation, and an ever-changing workforce, today's successful leader energizes and mobilizes all of the resources at his or her disposal to maximize opportunities and move the organization forward.

Being a leader today requires both a high intelligence quotient and a high emotional quotient. It's less about where the leader earned an MBA and more about what he or she has learned about getting the best from people and understanding how important they are to an organization's success. While a command of the "hard" skills of leadership is essential—such as business acumen, financial savvy, and vision—it is not until a leader masters the "soft" skills of leading people that he or she evolves into a complete leader.

Last, it is our hope that as a leader, you will share your wisdom and knowledge with those who come after you. True leadership prepares the way for future leadership. The world is in need of more authentic leaders—not just bosses or managers, but men and women who can raise the performance of a team. If you can, you will be a leader whose legacy and impact will far outlast your tenure. It will be your greatest contribution.

Author Biographies

RENEE BELLAMY BOOTH, PH.D.

Renee Bellamy Booth of Leadership Solutions, Inc. is an industrial organizational psychologist specializing in leadership assessment, coaching, development, and motivation. Her clients include the University of Pennsylvania, the Steinhardt and Tisch schools of New York University, the Vanguard Group, GE Life Sciences, Astellas Pharma, Biogen Idec, Lincoln Financial Group, the Financial Industry Regulatory Authority (FINRA), the Financial Accounting Foundation (FAF), the Financial Accounting Standards Board (FASB), Pennsylvania Real Estate Investment Trust, Bayer Diagnostics, CardioNet, The Investment Company Institute, and Cancer Treatment Centers of America. Dr. Booth's particular area of expertise is in supporting leaders to achieve organizational objectives through people effectiveness strategies, such as executive assessment, development, executive team building, and coaching interventions.

Prior to founding Leadership Solutions, Inc. in 1999, Dr. Booth was a general manager and vice president for the Hay Group, where she spent twelve years. In addition, she was the eastern regional practice leader for the Human Capital Group of Watson Wyatt Worldwide. In these positions, she was responsible for building and leading human resources practices to advance the organizations' strategic goals. Dr. Booth also held the position of senior vice president of corporate human resources for ADVANTA Corporation, a financial services company in the Philadelphia area, from 1996 to 1998.

Dr. Booth holds a bachelor's degree in psychology from the University of Maryland at College Park. She received her PhD in industrial/organizational psychology from Pennsylvania State University in 1986. Dr. Booth has published articles in *Pharmaceutical Executive* and *Personnel Psychology*. She is a member of the board of directors of Kenexa Corporation (a human resources software organization) and the Franklin Institute. She chairs the compensation committee of the board for both Kenexa Corporation and the Franklin Institute. She has also been a guest lecturer at the University of Pennsylvania's Wharton School of Business, Pennsylvania State University, Temple University, North Carolina Central University, Leadership Philadelphia, and numerous other professional organizations. She continues to be a guest speaker on leadership at corporate conferences and meetings within the region.

KEITH R. WYCHE

Known as a turnaround expert, Keith Wyche is the former president of ACME Markets (a division of Supervalu). In this role, he was responsible for the operations of the division office as well as the approximately 113-store, full-service retail and pharmacy chain based in the Philadelphia area with over $2 billion in sales. Wyche began his career in sales, marketing, and management roles with AT&T and IBM. Later, he served as president of US operations for Pitney Bowes Management Services.

Wyche is an author of two books, including his award-winning *Good Is Not Enough*, published in 2008 by Portfolio Press (a division of Penguin USA). Keith has been featured in a number of publications, including *Time*, *The New York Post*, *Diversity Inc.*, and *Black Enterprise*. In 2011, he was named CEO of the Year by the Executive50 organization. Morehouse College named him to the MLK International Board of Renaissance Leaders in 2008.

He is on the board of directors for WMS Industries and serves as vice chair of the National Black MBA Association. Keith earned his BBA from Cleveland State University and his MBA from Baldwin Wallace University.

CPSIA information can be obtained at www.ICGtesting.com
Printed in the USA
LVOW07s1634120215

426800LV00001B/295/P

9 780615 738222